BENCH OF DESPAIR

ഇൗരു

Dallas Smith

©2016
Nightengale Press
NIGHTENGALE MEDIA LLC

BENCH OF DESPAIR

For information about Nightengale Press
please visit our website at www.nightengalemedia.com.
Email: publisher@nightengalepress.com

Smith, Dallas,
BENCH OF DESPAIR/ Dallas Smith
ISBN 13: 978-1-935993-76-6
Sports/Ultra Marathon

First Published by Nightengale Press in the USA

April 2016

10 9 8 7 6 5 4 3 2 1

Printed in the USA, Canada, European Union, United Kingdom, France, Germany, Australia, Russia, Brazil, South Korea, Poland

Foreword

Meet the Devil

I've seen everything imaginable
Pass before these eyes
I've had everything that's tangible
Honey you'd be surprised
　　　　　　　—Guns 'N Roses, *Rocket Queen*

Sin.

Sin brought you to this godforsaken place that people confuse for a race. Sin is what you will do in every step of it, seeking some sort of transformation, redemption, or cleansing that you only curse and punt further down the road while you chase wild dogs back into their dens with vile oaths and curses.

Your intentions were pure. This race is not and neither are you. You walked off a peaceful ferry ride into hell.

Pure intentions might have existed in the planning stages that led you here, but you know without a doubt now that you are being punished for something major. The worst part is you can't escape it. Every step makes it worse.

You've lost hope because there is no hope. Death is going to find you and lay you out flat on that scorching Tennessee asphalt—to a fate no better than all the roadkill you've stepped on and tripped over in running as far as you have. You've become a domesticated kitty that you thought deserved a better fate than a wild animal hard-wired for survival. In the end, you discover you're just a plush teddy bear made in China. The road kills! The road doesn't discriminate, one of the few remaining vessels of the Southland that doesn't.

Babies will be born, hundreds of thousands of people will die, the weekend and a complete work week will pass and you'll still be hugging the shoulder of a crowded road, looking for a guard rail to sit on, a rest for your body and soul, all the while wondering why you hate yourself. That distant Willie Nelson song will cue your thought process to rue a bleak reality, "It's not the good life, but it's my life." It feels like the epitome of freedom and hell at the same time. You are as free as a lightning bug in July, but your tail is on fire and there's no off switch.

There is a saying that goes something like, "If you want to figure out who you really are then run a marathon." If you want to meet the slinking devil, then run the Vol State 500k. You'll meet this devil in McKenzie, Parker's Crossroads, Pelham, Jasper and several places in between. You'll have coffee with him in the morning, cuss him at high noon, punch him in the teeth at 3 am, and make deals with him around the clock.

The first three days of this race rabid dogs run at you, the last days of it they run from you. There are two reasons for this, one being that you are beyond disgusting and absolutely unappetizing, and secondly because you have no fear of them anymore. Because you don't care what happens to you. A man without fear is just as dangerous as a wild dog.

Naresh Kumar, extreme world explorer, summed it up perfectly in the midst of his lone Vol State 500k, telling the race's creator:

"Laz, I wish a truck would just hit me, not hard enough to kill me but just to injure me enough to knock me out of the race. Then competitors would have sympathy for my tragic luck, and I could leave the race as a hero."

Naresh wasn't so lucky. Trucks would see Naresh and almost veer into oncoming traffic to avoid him. No truck in the entire state wanted his raunch shell of a frame on its windshield.

That meant Naresh had to keep marching towards The Rock. He finished The Last Annual Vol State 500k, but he wasn't the same for nearly two years afterwards. Three days into the race I witnessed him pouring blistery fluids out of his Vibram Five Finger rubber-toed, foot condom shoes in Hohenwald, Tennessee. FYI: Condoms don't do well in extreme heat, especially between a rock and a hard place for over 314 miles. The damage was so severe that he refused to remove the Vibrams from his feet the last three days of the race. He feared he wouldn't be able to get them back on and that the visual of the damage he had inflicted would make him pass out.

In the end you realize you are the devil. You did this to yourself. People might applaud you, but they'll never understand you, and half of them will never believe you.

Sin.

—*Joshua Holmes*

Introduction

Spanish Inception

My sneakers pad the dust on a farm road in northern Spain, a segment of el Camino de Santiago, a pilgrim trail from France to the tomb of Saint James in western Spain. The sun hums with heat, hanging low in the west. I trudge toward it like walking into the fire. My Spanish friend, Albino Jimenez, has run on ahead. I am left alone without a telephone in a land where I barely speak the language. The dust is like talcum.

I'm finished. I've known it a while. The heat and the lack of food ruined me. We ran across the Pyrenees and landed in Pamplona, Spain on the first day—the same time a massive heat wave engulfed the northern region. Pamplona was the hottest town in the country, 104 degrees Fahrenheit.

It got worse. Today as we passed through Logroño we saw 107 on a thermometer. I couldn't get the food I needed. Finally, I couldn't keep down the food I found, spitting up even a Coke at an outdoor café today where a Frenchman sat beside the door smoking a joint. Albino is thirty years younger than I am. He is stronger. He has gone on.

I'll not make it to the hotel we booked in Nájera for tonight. It won't happen. What will happen? What will I do? How will I get there? I expect no ride. Two men on a tractor have passed. They were unfriendly and only glared when I waved.

I walk into the quiet little village of Ventosa. On Main Street I find the albergue, a hostel for pilgrims. A kind middle-aged woman is in attendance. She sizes me up and then turns on the fountain and fills my water bottle. I speak in halting Spanish:

"My friend and I are running el Camino. We started in Saint Jean. My friend ran ahead of me. But I no can run more. Can you call a taxi?"

She did. I surrendered. The taxi drove me to the hotel. The driver ripped me off when I didn't have the right change. I was too weak to fight—or to care.

Albino arrived a couple hours later. I had to tell him I'd quit. It was like slashing my wrists with a rusty knife. We'd planned the run a long time. It was a dream we'd held.

The next morning, I watched Albino set out on that day's run. Then, I caught a bus to Burgos, where his apartment was. Once there, I was so weak, I hurt my back. Two days later, Albino joined me at his house. He made an appointment with a doctor and gave up, too. We both had health problems.

That run was in June, 2009. It remains my most outstanding running failure. It worried me for years. I'd not just let myself down, I'd let Albino down, too. I felt like my quitting had led to his failure also. The moment for us to do that run has now passed. I knew I'd never have another chance at it.

Then around 2012 I became aware of the Vol State

500k, mostly through the stories of Tennessee-based running friends—Diane Taylor, Naresh Kumar, Joshua Holmes and Charlie Taylor. It sounded very much like the ad hoc run Albino and I'd tried to do in Spain. Although a couple hundred miles shorter, it happens in July, in the heat of summer, like we'd experienced in Spain.

I began to see Vol State as a chance for redemption. It wasn't el Camino, but it was close enough. And the course ran mostly through Tennessee, practically my backyard.

I signed up.

The pressure was on. July 2013 would be a moment of truth. It was a chance for redemption. But that's all it was, a chance. Success was not assured. I trained right down to the tiny details. I decided two things: I'd go at a safe pace and not push for speed. And, second decision, I'd write a brief blog post each night.

The run passed well. It was arduous enough all right. But I didn't experience threatening problems. I came to feel that it had been pretty easy, after all. In fact, I bragged that three words never appeared in my posts: "pain," "misery" and "suffer." And I said I had no injuries and wasn't sore. I noted a loss of weight but crowed about how nothing less than eating would cure that.

Do you see what was happening? Confidence is a wonderful thing. Over-confidence is dangerous. The line between the two is where you put it. Place it carefully.

I signed up in 2015 to run Vol State again. I figured I'd go faster than before. No sweat. I knew how to do it now. I blithely neglected things that had happened to me in the interim. I'd suffered a bout of Grave's disease. Doctors had prescribed a handful of pills, a variety that continually changed. By July 2015, race month, Grave's was in remission and pill-taking had vanished except for the garden variety old men usually take, like aspirin, statin and blood pressure pills. I ignored any detraining effect the layoff might have brought. I was ready to go again—I thought

The second running did not pass well. It was awful. I struggled to finish. My condition grew desperate as the days mounted. I redefined my mental and physical limits. I approached breakdown. It was like el Camino again, a novel in its denouement returning to the beginning. In the end, I finished—but barely.

The experience seared. The feeling lingered long after the race ended. I didn't intend to write about it, which requires, in some measure, reliving it. I *didn't* write about it. Months passed and I successfully avoided the issue. I wanted it behind me.

Then an editor invited me to write a piece for a literary magazine. I cut out a little slice of Vol State I thought I could use. That tiny piece grew and pulled me in until I wrote the whole story, the one you can read on the following pages.

First though, I need to say one other thing: I'm not an ultrarunner. I always deny I am. Obviously, I've run ultras. Vol State certainly qualifies. I run one occasionally for the adventure. That's my excuse. I'm not good at it. Any modest running success I've found has come at the traditional road distances, from 5k to marathon. Beyond those, I flounder.

In Vol State, unwittingly, I was taking a muscle-eating medicine. That singular fact added a level of mystery and drama I'd not counted on. Or maybe I'm just making a whiny excuse. Who knows?

Contents

*To Jo Ann, who enables my running
and endures my writing.*

*"I would rather die a robust death
than live a half-assed life."*

—*Alain Robert*

Chapter One

Meat Wagon Denied

Our back is to the water.

We stand on a two-lane pavement that angles gently into the flood behind us, drawing the eye along as it slides deeper and deeper, the double yellow line fading and finally disappearing in the murky depth. We smile for the camera, my phone actually. Bill Baker is holding it and making a group photo of the members of the Run It Fast running club that have shown up for The Last Annual Vol State 500k. There are twelve of us, thirteen counting Bill, a member too, but he's crewing and not running. Two more members will join us a bit later.

The race will have to start here, in Hickman, Kentucky. The Mississippi is too high for the ferry to operate. It can't take us to Dorena Landing, Missouri, the traditional starting place. This road goes to where the ferry would normally be moored. That place sets far out in the reach of the wide water today.

Altogether, there are eighty runners. Twenty-four have a crew, but the other fifty-six must find their own water, food and shelter as they travel along. That takes time and the clock is always running. The group is considerably larger than it has traditionally been. Two years earlier, when I first ran it, the group numbered forty-three. In years prior to that it was even smaller.

We mill around, sometimes standing, sometimes sitting on the pavement, simulating the traditional ferry ride to Dorena Landing. The race usually starts at 7:30 a.m.

I spot a tall white-bearded man, who I figure must be Don Winkley. He was once King of the Road, the winner. I also know he is seventy-seven years old. So, I walk up to him.

"You're the only person here keeping me from being the oldest runner," I say.

That's true, if maybe a bit impertinent. At seventy-five, I'm the second oldest. Don, however, is a crewed runner, whereas I am self-supported, thus the oldest unsupported runner here. But more, if I finish, I will become the oldest unaided runner to have ever finished this race. I am aware of that, and of course it's a goal. That goal lies yet 314 miles away. Nobody but me cares about that score.

Sometimes you're not in the mood for socializing. I'm not now. My sleep was awful last night. It was like I'd taken some kind of diuretic and my body was dehydrating as fast as it possibly could. I had to keep getting up to go to the bathroom, even had leg cramps—also a sign of dehydration in my case. Was it something I ate? I need to sleep. Starting this race already punked out, I don't want to talk.

I miss the ferry boat ride. I remember it from two years ago. It carried the runners, as well as two pickup trucks, over to Missouri. In crossing, I found a visitor register in a glass-fronted cabinet, the kind of book you sign to show you were there. Apparently, runners had never noticed it before.

Hey, we need to sign this.

I showed the book to race director, Lazarus Lake. It was a discovery. He signed it and then all the other runners signed it, too. I wanted to sign that register again.

The boat had a two-man crew. I asked one, a young man, about the boat's propulsion. He told me the boat had two marine John Deere engines governed down to 367 Horsepower each. It's good to have plenty of power on that wide river.

Once the boat landed in Missouri, all the runners disembarked and walked up the bank sixty yards or so, and stood there behind an invisible starting line marked by a utility pole, I think. Race director, Lazarus Lake, didn't start the race by firing a pistol or blowing a horn. No, instead he started it by flicking a flame and lighting a cigarette. We took off trotting down the bank and jumped back on the boat, leaving him standing there in a cloud of smoke.

The boat, which had taken us to Missouri in the first place, then took us back to Hickman. After we'd landed in Kentucky and everyone had rushed off ,except *Running Journal* columnist, Ray Krolewitz and me, I told him I want to be the last off and motioned him forward. "I do, too," he said. I don't know if he'd thought about it before then. Anyway we agreed to a compromise and hit Kentucky soil in lock-step, tied for last place. That was two years ago. Today, there's no boat ride. Runners hangout on the Hickman pavement.

I feel mean and low. I drift down to the water's edge and find Thomas Skinner, an affable man from Georgia. He and I shared a hotel room last night in Union City, a town nearby that the race director uses for a staging area the night prior to the race. He makes the hotel reservations for us there, and if you're a loner like I am, he matches you up with a roommate. We also have a group dinner there, ironically referred to as the Last Supper.

I knew the name of the man I'd be matched with, but I only met him yesterday, at breakfast in Kimball, Tennessee. That town is on the other end of the course, just fourteen miles from the finish line at Castle Rock, Georgia. Several of us spent the night there and left our cars in Castle Rock and rode a charter bus from there to here. Actually, it took two buses, as large as the group has grown. So, yesterday before our bus ride, I sat down with a stranger at breakfast in the Super-8 at Kimball. It turned out to be Thomas Skinner. We each met our roommate at that moment.

"I got your book!" he said.

"Oh, you do? Thanks, which one?" I wasn't expecting anyone to even know I write books.

Anyway, this morning I find Thomas sitting patiently near the water, waiting like everyone else. We chat a bit. No need to get excited. I put my pack down for a pillow, as I will many times in days ahead, and go to sleep. I could have slept a long time, but didn't.

"Wake up, Dallas! The race's started."

It's Thomas giving me a wake-up. I roll my head and watch him trot off, jump up, snap on my pack, and head

out. That's the casual and unlikely way I start this imposing piece of business.

We head toward the center of Hickman. Then to com-
pensate for the mileage we missed in riding the boat over
to Dorena, we make a turnaround and head back toward
the river. At the water we make another turnaround and
head toward Hickman Centro again. In that last turn, I
swipe my hand through the river water.

Good-bye, Big River.

Finally, now this operation is under way and we get
strung out along the road going into Hickman.

Hickman is a small river town, and it doesn't take
long to run through it. Five miles will do it. Here's a market, about the last you see of Hickman. I filled my bottles
here two years ago. This time I'm in better shape, carrying
three bottles, instead of two. Odd thing, at this point in the
run last time, two motorists had already stopped me to ask
directions. I wasn't any help. I'd never been here before. All
I knew was what my little stack of five-by-six-inch maps
told me.

John Price, the expert of this race, put the maps online
free of charge for that purpose. I'd downloaded, printed
and trimmed them, and was carrying them in plastic bags.
I'm carrying the very same maps again this time. I always
obsess about making a wrong turn. The maps are worth
gold.

John has done a lot to help runners in this race. He
wrote a booklet that tells where runners can expect to find
a market, a hotel—or even places with vending machines
setting outside and hence available even in the middle of

the night. I left the booklet at home, paring my load to a minimum.

John has twice crossed America from ocean to ocean. He has run this race some eight times now. On two occasions he double-ran it. After finishing in Georgia, he turned and ran the course in reverse, back to the start. On one of those occasions, a tornado in West Tennessee disrupted his return run. On this stretch of road, from Hickman to Union City, John gave me, the greenhorn, a good tip: "Most of the damage is done in the first day," he said. I took that advice seriously when he said it, and I still do.

You'd think you wouldn't have to kill yourself. Do the math. The distance is 314 miles and you have ten days to officially finish. That's only 31.4 miles per day. Of course, if you're an unaided runner, at the end of that thirty-one-mile stretch, there may be no place to eat or sleep. You have to keep going. Some days will necessarily be longer than others. So, the run can't be as uniform and well-ordered as the arithmetic suggests.

This stretch of road, Hickman to Union City, Tennessee, is not hard, only annoying. You'd never expect so many people to have urgent business in Hickman. Traffic is heavy, including trailer trucks and no paved shoulder to escape on. I have to step off the pavement onto a dirt shoulder covered by grass and weeds. It slopes away, which causes my foot to slip sideways in my shoe. Too much of that can cause a blister. Take it easy. Avoid damage on the first day.

The Last Annual Vol State Road Race, as this event is officially and jokingly called—it's only "last" until the next one—typically begins on the second Thursday of July, deep in the heart of July's heat, not the best time for running. Everything about the race is ironic, from its distance of 314 miles—"One Hundred Pi," as runners like to kid— to July's heat, to its finish line just inches from a 100-foot precipice. It's all crazy. It's meant to be.

The race was created and is directed by Gary Cantrell, aka, Lazarus Lake, which name I mentioned before, noted for having created the Barkley Marathons, a race designed to make you fail. It succeeds. Last I knew, only fourteen humans had ever finished it, all men. Also among Cantrell's creations is the Strolling Jim forty-mile ultramarathon in his hometown of Wartrace, Tennessee, a race named after a dead horse and a race whose length is not, in fact, forty miles but instead 41.2. Laz, as we call him, finds great humor in irony.

Vol State has mushroomed in the last three years from a dozen or two hardcore ultrarunners to eighty this year. Two years ago, only forty solo runners started, half as many as now. The year before that, fifteen.

The race in its present form started in 2006. There was one finisher that year. John Price told me in an e-mail of July 22, 2013, that 2006 was the first year the distance was ten times 50k. Before then it was ten times the marathon distance for a few years, then random distances and courses.

It's interesting to consider the number to finish each year. Lumping aided and unaided runners, I've noted the number in parentheses for given years: 2006(1); 2007(3); 2008(4); 2009(12); 2010(6); 2011(13); 2012(14); 2013(33); and

2014(45). It will turn out that the current year, 2015, will see fifty-nine finishes. Adding them all up, the total number of finishes, through the current year, comes to only 190. The number of runners is a bit less, since some runners finished more than once. Regardless, 190 finishes in a ten year period is not many. Vol State appeals to a rare breed of runners.

In the jokey lexicon of Vol State, the two categories of aided and unaided runners are referred to as "crewed" and "screwed." Aided runners are permitted a crew to bring supplies such as food and drink and air-conditioned transportation to a hotel or restaurant.

An unaided runner can only accept drinks and food from random strangers and from other unaided runners, but is allowed no planned help. If an unaided runner ever gets in or on a moving conveyance, even if it doesn't take him forward, even if it takes him backwards, in that moment he becomes a crewed runner, even though he has no actual crew.

Those are the rules. Most runners choose to run unaided, seeking the transcendent experience of total self-reliance. Self-reliance and the timely kindness of strangers, that's it, 314 miles on your own. Here I am trying to do it again. Can I?

Oh, one other thing: Laz requires that each runner carry a small American flag attached to clothes or pack. It serves as a race bib, he says. It may also have the helpful effect of assuring people we meet along the way that we're patriots rather than crooks, terrorists or homeless drunks— which we may come to resemble as the miles wear on us.

It will come to seem that the road goes on forever—

and the clock never stops. The last part is right. The clock never stops, not until precisely 240 hours have expired. The road ends, however, atop a ledge in Georgia they call "The Rock."

That is all very far away from me now and out of mind. Today, I'm trying to avoid damage. Today, I can look up and see a line of runners strung out up the road. It gets thinner the farther we go. After today, no line will be present, and I will be alone most of the time, only occasionally encountering another runner.

Sergio Bianchini is a runner I know from Chattanooga, and he's very good. At age seventy-four, he is barely younger than I am. This is his first attempt at this adventure. His inexperience shows: his pack is too big. I like to kid him about it. He is also running with two women from Chattanooga. Not sure how that works, either. There are complications. I'd rather be alone. Anyway, I come up on the three of them now, resting in the shade at the end of a bridge parapet. Sergio is wrestling with his pack balanced on the end of the parapet.

"What you got in there, Sergio, a chainsaw? How about a socket set?" Lynda and Betty, his two companions, laugh. They can see we're friends. I go on. We'll meet again.

I catch up to a woman I want to talk to. She has bright eyes and wears dread locks and represents a rarity in this backcountry-type of activity: she's black. That fact will assume some significance in this farm country before the day is over. We don't know that now. I spoke with her briefly yesterday during the ride when the bus stopped at a market. I tell her my name and I hear her say hers is "Camilla."

It will happen that before day's end I'll learn more.

We jog along, talking. She grew up in Brooklyn, but she got into trouble when she was seventeen. It was because of her boyfriend.

"They shot his car up and he got arrested."

"Was he in it?" I ask.

"Yeah, they shot him too, three times." She can't remember all the places where he was hit and she doesn't say who the shooters were. Maybe I'm supposed to assume police, I don't know.

"Were you with him?"

"Yeah."

"Did you get hit, too?"

"No."

It is one of those kinds of things that happens to young people sometimes.

"When you're seventeen, you're so in love. You are *soooo* in love." She says it with great stress, having learned from the episode. In very truth, she speaks the wisdom of experience. Kids have trouble growing up, city girl and country boy alike.

Things changed. That's why she's here today, headed toward Union City. Her parents had means. Her dad was an official in city government. They sent her to Georgia to live with her great grandmother. Did I hear that right?

"Your *great* grandmother, not just grandmother?"

"Yes, great grandmother."

Her great grandmother must have been a woman of great strength and wisdom. Camilla speaks of her with warm affection. Living with her changed Camilla. She

26

found her direction, went to college, got a degree, and she lives in Atlanta today. Her parents come down from New York to visit her and their grandchildren now.

Two people with backgrounds more different never ran side by side down the road talking. I'm old and she's young. I'm white, she's black. I was raised in the country, she in the city. I was born in a two-room log house and raised in the hills. The old doctor who attended my birth didn't bother to make a certificate of that fact. I went through college and was in graduate school before I ever got a birth certificate, a delayed one. My mother went to court, took the family Bible, where my birth was recorded, and got affidavits from those who'd known me from childhood, one from my grade-school teacher. Finally, The State of Tennessee mailed her official proof of my birth.

But Brooklyn, I know people from Brooklyn and I've walked around there and run through it and fell and bloodied my elbow there, but I have little idea what growing up there would be like. Camilla, I think would have equal trouble imagining what my life was like in the Depression-area Cumberland foothills where I was raised. We can each learn from the other.

The conversation turns to running. Camilla isn't dressed the way I'd expect. In this July heat, for example, she has on a hot-looking fuzzy hat, a sort of thick beanie. Her pack is huge. The handle of a scabbard knife pokes out of her bra. I wonder if she's thought deeply about this run. Truth is, I really don't know this run either. I'm a greenhorn at multi-day events. The runners around me vary a lot in approach, style, mode of dress and so on. One woman I

27

talked with earlier was wearing a Panama hat. I thought it looked very stylish.

Take John Sharp, a gentleman I remember from our wait this morning. His build reminds me more of a running back than an endurance runner—strong, stoutly built, low center of gravity. He could bench-press my pickup truck. Far from the grim ascetic you'd expect, he's also an irrepressible talker, who always seems to be telling a story with a humorous ending. He laughs a lot. If you told him his house had burned down, he'd only pause long enough to make a quip and then go on with his story, funny party talk. Ultrarunners often don't look like runners, I've learned.

Drifting along, Camilla smacks me with an unexpected statement I have to ask about twice: She ran seventy-five miles on Sunday.

"What? Seventy-five on Sunday?" This is just Thursday! Normally, you don't do a long training run so close to a race. For just a marathon, you'd leave a two-week taper period after the last long run, not four days. You ran seventy-five on Sunday?"

"Yeah, seventy-five."

Everybody surprises me. A run like this surprises you.

Camilla's name vaguely bothers me. I don't know why, maybe because I feel like I'm saying it wrong. My tin ears easily miss fine distinctions in sound. "Camilla" is the name of a flower, a pink delicate one that looks slightly like a rose. I have some growing at the foundation of our house. I know a woman named Camille. The "e" on the end is silent in her name. I never knew anyone named Camilla before. So, I ask her about it.

"Do you pronounce it like Ca-MILL-ah or more with a Spanish sound like Ca-MEE-yah?"

"Yeah, like that," she replies. That's the short answer. I'd learn a better one.

I don't want to bother anyone's run, so eventually, I leave her and go ahead, working my way toward Union City. I'm looking forward to lunch, which I plan to have there. Good reason, there's a Subway restaurant there, at the place where we turn left, a bench mark.

Once I arrive, some other Vol State runners are in Subway, including the indefatigable John Sharp. I learned a lesson here last time: I bought a sandwich the same time as John Price. I sat down to eat mine while he went out the door and ate his strolling down the sidewalk. Once I'd finished, I went outside and discovered John had gotten far ahead, even though he was going slowly. That example showed me the importance of "relentless forward motion," as it's been called. It's a lesson, but it's a lesson I often neglect, being too fond of talking.

This time I don't talk, but instead head out the door with a sandwich, following John Price's example. I don't know if lunch requires extra fluid or to what extent my rushed lunch undoes me. Because a mile later, I suddenly discover that I am severely dehydrated. Given the leg cramps last night, a symptom of dehydration onset, I should have been drinking more fluids than normal this morning. Instead, I've drunk less, I realize. It's a tendency with me, being casual and cavalier. The cost is high. Before leaving Union City, I pay up.

Both legs cramp hard, thighs, calves and feet, all the leg muscles I use to run. The failure is catastrophic and massive, as if every muscle snatches into all the tension it is capable of exerting. The pain is a lake of fire. The paralysis is complete. I teeter a moment, like Sadam's statue, a rigid body leaning, leaning more. As I topple, a maroon car passes going toward town.

I can do nothing, except lie rigid like I fell, grinding my teeth, clenching my fists at my side, a keening sound like *eeeewww* coming from my throat. It takes a while doing that. Time drags, exquisite pain hums. Inquisition: green wood, slow burning, engulfing flames, melting flesh, keening rising like smoke, *eeeewww*.

It's the nightmare I've often had about this kind of run. Now it's happening.

It's happened twice before, the most awful time on a marathon in Morocco. My buddy Albino Jimenez was running beside me that day. He held me upright in a bear hug until I could stand and eventually try to walk. After that the going was slow. I began drinking bottles of water to recover. The trudging walk continued. Our projected finishing time put catching our flight to Spain in jeopardy. The water helped, but I could walk only very slowly. We agreed Albino should go on and check out of our hotel and then come back for me. That was the only chance to catch the flight. I watched him disappear ahead. I was left alone in an alien culture and unfamiliar place scarcely able to walk. At least there was plenty of water on the course. My body soaked it up like a parched desert. I counted how many bottles I drank as I shuffled forward. After eight, walking became a bit more comfortable. I finally recovered enough to run the last three miles.

It was a close call. After Albino found me in the crowd, we headed to the Casablanca airport, pushing the taxi driver to go fast. I had no chance to shower or change clothes. In the taxi, I pulled street clothes on over my sweaty running duds. That was how I rode the plane to Madrid—and then rode the car 150 miles on to Burgos, Albino's home. Decked out in dank clothes, but no longer cramping.

Now, I lay on the ground in Tennessee, silent now, the muscle spasm relaxing gradually. After a while I decide to risk sitting upright. I can push with my arms. They don't cramp. I've been lying on my waist bottle. It's nearly full. The other two are empty. I sit, my legs splayed out. I don't dare move them.

What in hell am I going to do?

I find some salt packs in my shorts' pocket, which may help. I eat the salt and drink the whole bottle of water. After another wait, I gingerly risk getting my legs back underneath me and succeed in standing. I test one careful step, then another and slowly begin to work my way along the sidewalk.

Even though she saw the old man fall, the woman in the maroon Mercury kept going. She was driving her teen-aged daughter to town. But the incident worried her, the guy falling for no apparent reason and then lying there without moving. It seemed *final.* She turned around and drove back. She saw now that he'd gotten up and was walking gingerly along the walk toward a gravel drive that crossed it. She turned the car into the drive and stopped astraddle the walk just as he walked up. What she said was what he would hear over and over in the days ahead:

"Are you okay?"

"Yes, thanks, my legs cramped. I'm better now."

"I saw you fall. It scared me. I came back."

"Thanks, I believe I'll be okay. I ate some salt and drank some water. I let myself get dehydrated. That causes cramps."

"Well, do you need anything?"

"I guess not. It's happened before. I know what to do. I just have to take it easy. I'll get better."

"I was headed into town. I saw you fall. It scared me!"

"Scared me, too."

She backs out and heads toward town, as I realize I didn't ask her for any water. I'm out of water and never once thought to ask for any.

Shit! I've got to have water.

I hobble on up the walk. Soon I come to a frame house close to the walk, and I step up on the porch and knock on the wood. A young woman comes to the door. I tell her I'm running cross country and ask her if she'll fill my bottle. She leaves and brings it back full.

I should have let her fill all three bottles, but I hope to come to a market where I can get more water. There's a problem with that plan. I soon realize I'm leaving town and there are no additional markets. I continue to hobble across a landscape that grows more and more rural. And there's no place to find water.

Now Camilla catches me and she slows to my hobbling pace for a while. I tell her about my legs cramping

32

and how I fell. She's rocking right along, not bothered by any of the troubles I have, so I let her go on. No need to stay back with me.

I've been expecting this scene, and now I see it: Lazurus Lake and his partner Carl Laniack, sitting in the shade of an overpass. They want to write down our time for the twenty-mile distance—or for whatever distance it is, counting or not counting the ferry boat ride which we didn't take. Anyway, here they sit with pencil and paper. And Laz says,

"She said you fell, Dallas."

"Well, yeah, but that wasn't the real problem. I got dehydrated and my legs cramped so hard I fell down. It's leg cramps that I'm battling."

Fall, my eye.

I go on thinking. Fall is nothing compared to the leg cramps. But most people don't know that. I still have not found water, and I'm nearly out again. I have to have water to go on. I have to go on to find water. It's the old egg-chicken conundrum. Everybody's catching me now, and salvation is at hand from a very unexpected source. John Sharp catches me, together with a couple of buddies. Here he comes with his shiny metal hiking poles, and you hear him talking and laughing a long time before he pulls alongside and asks the old question,

"You doing okay?'

"Yeah, I got dehydrated and my legs cramped. I had to slow down."

"You need some water?"

"Well, I'm just about out. Maybe I can find some

ahead."

"Here take this bottle!"

"Oh, thanks man, but I don't want to take your water. You may need it."

"No, we got plenty. Our bladders packs are full. This is just extra. Here, take it, this one, too."

It's a timely gift. I owe John Sharp. He gives me a bottle and a half. That gets me a little further down the road, just far enough to find Camilla. She's got her shapely leg propped on a bridge handrail massaging out a Charley Horse, a cramp. She has run nearly out of water, too. And she has a small-scale case of what I had a lot of. It may get worse. We have gone at different paces in various places. And now we've both arrived at this same place, and in the same condition, our fates entwined in the same jeopardy.

We go marching down the road together in search of water. Are we going to run out of ability to march before we find water? That's the question. This is farm country, soy beans and corn fields, not many houses. No runners are in sight, front or back now. Camilla and I trudge along in, what has become for me, anyway, a desperate search.

I am more compromised by dehydration than she is. She's stronger.

If we don't find water soon, I'm going to be on the roadside unable to move. There is a volunteer named Jan Walker who will take care of that situation. Jan drives a van referred to as the meat wagon. It is the dark maroon color of dried blood. Jan will put me in her van. My race will be over. Through. Kaput. DNF. She will drive me back to my car in Georgia, in defeat, despair and disgrace. There, I will tuck my tail tight over my diminished manhood and slink toward home like a whipped hound, dogged all the way by a single thought.

I didn't even make it to Martin.

Only it's worse than that. Jan's drive likely will not be so direct. It will be slow and drawn out. It might take a day or two, because there'll be other failures to pick up. She has to work it out as riders accumulate. We may have to spend a night sleeping in the van. We'll be a sad wagon.

I would kill myself to finish a race. By that, I mean I'll go past reasonable limits of health and danger. I've known this for a long time, that I'd kill myself to finish. I hope I do someday. I hope today is not that day. I have to find water soon.

There is a sense of unease I feel about this situation—besides the water. I am a white guy, albeit an old one, walking with a comely black woman along a rural road, both lightly dressed in shorts. I know how that looks to a racist. I grew up with racists. I was a racist. I grew up in Tennessee when it was accepted behavior and I could not have known otherwise.

The South has changed. People are more enlightened now. There is not much open racism anymore. But there are still pockets of it. Only a month before this race, a Confederate-flag-waving racist slaughtered nine black worshipers in a Charleston, South Carolina church, purely because they were black. That kind of violence comes to mind as you trod these roads. The potential is still here.

On this run we'll see the Confederate battle flag flying high on a pole in a front yard, or flapping in the wind behind a pickup cab. Those flag owners aren't necessarily racists. They may only be celebrating their family's culture, as they would likely say. Others, though, look like bullies itching for a fight. It's ignorance. If you crossed out Robert E. Lee and Stonewall Jackson, they'd have trouble naming another Confederate general.

Tennessee, the whole South for that matter, has not crawled completely out of the backwoods I grew up in. That fact still affects how I feel, how I react, always a little on guard. I've lived in Tennessee, Virginia and Alabama, all southern states. I have two great granduncles, brothers, who died in the Civil War fighting for the South, one at Atlanta of measles, one at Murfreesboro while he was planting the flag on the enemy battery. My maternal grandmother told me this about her uncles.

My paternal grandfather had the same uncles. So, these fallen soldiers come from lineage of both my parents. My father and mother were second cousins, sharing the same great-grandparents. Let us all now make jokes about inbreeding. I expect it *was* common. People lived out their lives where they were born, having a limited circle of friends and acquaintances.

I acknowledge and honor the sacrifices of my ancient uncles and I applaud their valor. But, in the end, they were chumps, misguided and in the wrong place at the wrong time. They likely thought they were fighting for their homeland. In fact, they were poor white boys fighting to give rich white men the right to keep black people like livestock.

Don't tell me about how your family's Civil War history entitles you to taunt others with the Confederate flag. I don't agree. My family has history here too, in this bloody land where I choose to live. I've thought about moving from the South, about going to live elsewhere. In the end, if it's true that one votes with his feet, I've cast my ballot: I still live in the South. I reckon I'll make my last stand here.

That last stand is at hand if Camilla and I don't find water. We come to a house. It's a frame house that sets in a field lower than the road. It's safer if I knock.

"You wait here, Camilla," I say, "I'll see if I can raise anybody. If I can fill my bottles, I'll come back and get yours."

I shuffle down the embankment and across the yard. Water stands in the grass at places. Ironically, I dodge puddles on my search for water. I step up on the porch and knock hard. That sets off a dog inside. He blasts the alarm, screaming assault and home invasion, and he doesn't let up. No one comes to the door. Probably at work.

We have to go on. A little further and we make out a broad building on our right. From the disabled cars around it, it looks like a country car-care place. A sign:

"Does that say 'Transmissions'? You can probably see better than me," I tell Camilla.

"Yeah, that's it."

"Well, we gotta try it."

Camilla knows that.

It is the kind of place where you'd not be surprised to find three drunk rednecks driving a jacked-up Dodge Ram—and maybe acting the way I've been thinking about. The door of the building is open, a dark rectangle. It's my job to take the lead. My Tennessee accent and kindly white beard hold the better chance. I march in, Camilla trailing.

The room is dark and dusty. Five people huddle loosely around a worn brown counter, three good ole boys, a slender old man and a white haired woman, maybe a family holding a conference. The three younger men are likely brothers. No customers brother them. The old man and woman sit on this side, with one of the brothers, who is studying a computer screen. One brother is on the opposite side looking at a screen. One is up walking about. I hold up an empty bottle.

"Ya'll got a place where we can fill up our water bottles?"

It's quiet. They look at us. Camilla hangs back. We've interrupted.

Then, "How about some cold Gatorade?"

"That'd be great! That's better than water."

Two brothers go into the back and returned with Gatorade and water. I let one of the brothers pour me two bottles of Gatorade and one of water, thinking three bottles of sweet stuff might make me sick. The Gatorade has the electrolytes I likely need to recover. Another brother fills Camilla's bottles. The walking-around-brother is the oldest. He has a nervous tick that makes his face scrunch when he speaks.

I tell them how we are running across Tennessee and that we'd both run out of water and gotten leg cramps. Camilla had taken a tattered chair near the door.

"Camilla, here, is from Atlanta. I live in Tennessee. We were running out of ability to keep going. We ought to be fine now."

"It's hot, ya'll need to be careful."

"I know I can't pay you." I dig a limp ten dollar bill out of my shorts. "But let me leave a donation for your favorite charity or church collection plate." I hold the bill out. Nobody will take it.

"No, we're glad to help. We don't want any money for it. Just be careful and have a good run. We like to help."

I thank them again. The white-haired old lady faces us on her stool.

"God bless, both ya'll," she says.

With that, she specifically includes Camilla. They'd filled Camilla's bottles as quickly as they had the old Tennessean's. We leave with our bottles full. As we walk away, I am struck by how kind they'd been, how they'd helped us without hesitation, both of us. I am grateful and amazed.

"Those good ole boys helped us. It makes me proud. It makes me proud of Tennessee, corny as that sounds. I'm amazed how good they were. Sometimes you find good people. They were good people." Camilla nods and echoes my sentiments.

They saved us from the meat wagon.

The water helps me recover. Soon, I'm able to go a bit faster and I leave Camilla, who's probably tired of me hanging around anyway.

My plan is simple: Go short today. Martin is where I plan to spend the night, just thirty miles into the run. That plan is consistent with the idea of doing no damage on the first day. There is a hotel in Martin with fast food restaurants around it. I can have a regular sit-down meal.

This is the procedure: We report our position to Laz and Carl every twelve hours, at seven-thirty in the morning and night. Some people actually make a phone call, but I don't like to talk on a phone, so I always send a text instead. Everyone's position is then entered into a Google spreadsheet, which the public can view. A number of people at home fascinated by the race—or maybe having a friend in it—will follow our progress along the course. It shows our position both in a table and on a map.

The Vol State runners themselves are the ones most intensely interested in it. You want to see where your friends are, whether in front or behind. They may pass you while you're sleeping or in a market eating and you don't know it. I got shut out of the info last time I ran the race. Three days into the run, my phone somehow logged me out of Google and I couldn't remember the password to get back in. So, I knew little. After three days, so strung out were we, I only occasionally saw another runner.

After I'd checked into the hotel at Martin and had a shower, I eat a sandwich at Subway, which was nearly adjacent to the hotel. Second time in one day to eat at Subway.

I am anxious to see where Camilla has ended up. So, I search the update table. There is no Camilla. I scan over it again. My eye lands on Jameelah Adul-Rahim Mujaahid. Oh no! It's not Ca-MEE-lah, as I'd thought, it's Ja-MEE-lah! I've mispronounced her name all day long. I feel like a fool. That would be an *old* fool.

I must apologize. She's nine miles ahead of me now. I don't know when I'll see her again. Or if I'll see her again. I regret the error so much, and I wish I could tell her I'm sorry, but that chance may never come. It's just like other mistakes in life, some of them you can never correct.

Only thirty miles for me today. But, a full day doesn't end until seven-thirty tomorrow morning. I will have been running five hours by then, and twelve or fifteen miles further down the road. I'd better be.

One more chore: I decided some time ago that I'd write a blog post on Facebook each day. I did that the last time and several friends followed it. They came to look forward to each new installment. They told me so. It has immediacy. It becomes a serial of an ongoing story that you truly don't know the ending to. Even the writer doesn't. I try to make it brief, but you cannot call yourself a writer without being fussy about word choice and sentence structure. It takes me an hour, posting pictures and fat-finger typing on the little phone. That's an hour each day I could use sleeping or running, a big chunk of time. But I'm willing to give it up, whatever happens.

Last time I made this run, I was more careful. In light of all the dehydration and cramps I had today, it's interesting to look at a sentence I posted on this day two years ago:

Hydration and electrolytes went well. NO LEG CRAMPS! Tomorrow: up early, maybe go longer.

Chapter Two

Flaming Quads

Runners sleep everywhere. They curl up and sprawl out in cemeteries, on church porches, far corners of parking lots and even the woods. I prefer a bed. I prefer a bed after taking a shower. You get pretty rank running in the July heat, sweating like a pig. That's the cliché, although pigs can't sweat. That's why they love lying in mud.

But a hotel is a bad bargain. It seems a waste of money. You pay for the whole night, but you're soon gone again. Another factor is that if you are an unaided runner—the old "screwed" runner—you must actually get yourself to a place where there is a hotel. If you grow so exhausted you can't, then you'll sleep out for the night. That's not a problem an aided runner faces. His crew can seat him in an air-conditioned car and drive him to a hotel, so long as he comes back to the same place to start running again.

Waste or not, indulgent or not, I choose a hotel if possible. It's the cost of doing business.

Friday, I was out of my hotel at two-thirty in the morning running University Street through Martin, Tennessee. It is much better to run at night than in the heat of the day. The running is easier and a bottle of water goes further.

Momentarily, I set my pack on the walk to make an adjustment and, doing that, I saw a figure in a brisk walk approaching. So, I waited. It turned out to be Terrie Wurzbacher. At age sixty-five, she was trying to become the oldest woman to finish this race. She was supported by veteran Marvin Skagenburg. She tried it the previous year but dropped out, concluding she wasn't ready. But she came back to try it again. I hadn't met her before and I was glad for the company.

She doesn't look like a runner and she's not. She's a walker, at least she is in this adventure. That's okay. The secret is one doesn't have to run a step to finish this race. You can walk all the way, so long as you cover an average of 31.4 miles per day. Terrie and I drifted along together, under the street lamps, down the walk fronting Martin University. Then her phone rang.

"That's probably Marv," she said and stopped to talk.

I went on and never saw her again. But she did finish this time, I've learned.

I left Martin and headed toward Dresden. In leaving Martin, I passed underneath an overpass bridge. It was a landmark for me that triggered a memory from the other time I ran this race. I hadn't started out as early that day, and was passing under the bridge in the dawning. The sun was shining on the farmland long before I hit Dresden.

I wrote:

A lone pigeon cooed in the dark beams as I passed under a bridge at 5 a.m. At 6 a.m. the sun was barely up. It cast my shadow fifty yards long across the rows of a low soybean field. That thin wafting shadow measured my puny motion in precise 32-inch intervals.

But this time I passed under the bridge long before dawn. The pigeon was quiet. Soybean rows would not register my shadow's passing. Instead, the moon hung low in the east, rising just a bit before sunrise. Its rise would grow later in the days ahead, I knew, until it would disappear from the night sky altogether. That was a pity, because it's good to run by moonlight.

The sky was growing light as I entered Dresden. I threaded my way looking for water. A long stretch of countryside was waiting once I left town. I came to the Weakley County Library. It was much too early for anyone to be around. I walked all about the building and finally found a faucet in the back. I unscrewed the garden hose and filled my bottles and then screwed the hose back on so as to leave things the way I found them.

The route to Gleason was a rural two-lane, a country road. At places there were swamps on either side heavy with vegetation. Cottonmouths thick as a thigh would be lounging in there, I figured. It was on this small road where I remember seeing my first deceased armadillo two years earlier, victim of a traffic accident. It was only the first of many I'd see on that trip. Road-killed armadillos became cliché.

Armadillos have an unusual trait. When alarmed they spring straight up into the air. This served the useful purpose of startling and scaring their old enemies. Springing up is thus in their genes. It's no good now. Their new enemies are cars traveling at fifty-five miles per hour. The inherited behavior doesn't frighten a car. It merely guarantees a fatal collision with steel and plastic.

Trotting along I carry two sets of maps. One set shows the course, the other set shows details of the cities at a larger scale. It's not good enough to merely go into town and out the other side. You must follow the course shown on the map. It sometimes takes a tortuous path. In towns with a courthouse, it curves so as to pass that structure. Imagine running 314 miles and learning later you'd missed a couple of blocks of the course. You'd feel like your run was incomplete and tarnished. You'd be right. Racers can't take shortcuts.

Going into Gleason I was anxious. I wanted to get to the Korner Kafe, where I remembered having breakfast two years ago and I was looking forward to eating there again. I had my Gleason city map out and was looking for a left-hand turn.

Suddenly, a dog that looked like a black-and-white Jack Russel mix came charging into the road behind me, outraged that I'd have the nerve to run on his street. I looked back over my shoulder and kept going. A one-armed man dashed out and scooped up the mutt like a short stop, tucked him under his arm and rumbled back to the porch for a ten-yard gain like a fullback. No disability here.

And while I was watching that remarkable performance was precisely the moment I ran past my turn. Only I didn't know that. I kept going until I came to a Tee intersection and then went left. The street didn't look right, but I couldn't find a street sign for a long ways. Finally, a cross street that I could also find on my map showed I was off course. I had to backtrack to get back to the official route. Backtracking, once I reached the house where the belligerent little dog lived, I saw the street I needed. The dog had distracted me just enough to make me miss it. So, I ran a little extra. It wasn't far. The uncertainty made it seem longer, but it was probably less than a mile. It annoyed me because it delayed my arrival at the Korner Kafe.

I walked in and someone yelled, "Hey, look here!"

It was my old buddy Sergio, still together with his young friends Lynda and Betty. I made a picture. There he sat, already burned red from the sun, but beaming like an Italian stud, blond-headed Lynda's arm wrapped around his shoulder. Betty was in the restroom being sick. She had to drop out later that day. I warned him about running with those fast women. Look where he is now—ahead of me.

Then uber-marathon couple Cathie and Troy Johnson came in. They go everywhere and run marathons side-by-side. They had recently run seven marathons on seven continents in twelve days. Their goal had been to do it in seven days and they almost did. On the way to the last marathon, in Antarctica, I think it was, the plane had to turn back because of bad weather. They waited five days and then made it.

A reunion of sorts took place in the Korner Kafe. Then I split.

McKenzie was the next town. Once through it, the road to Huntingdon, where I meant to spend the night was a wide divided highway that rolled over low hills. It has absolutely no shade. I became aware of the heat. The afternoon sun was hot on my legs. You could feel the rays like standing too close to a stove. It would turn out that we'd have several consecutive days when the temperature index went past a hundred. I could have checked the temperature on my smart phone at any time. But I refused. It didn't matter with me. I was going to go on regardless, compromising little for heat. For the same reason, I never put ice in my water bottles, even when it was available at markets. I didn't want to train myself to want ice. I was determined: drive a hard bargain with myself. Make no concessions.

That attitude caught up with me on the Huntingdon stretch. I noticed my quadriceps burning, not just from the sun but from inside. I'd been pushing too hard for too long. My muscles were actually breaking down, taking damage as I ran. The front of my legs felt hot and feverish to the touch. It was distressing to have this happening. It was something new, too. I had to quit running and walk the rest of the way to Huntingdon.

After I finished the race, my doctor gave me a blood test that showed I'd been losing muscle. He told me that my cholesterol medicine contributed to the breakdown and that I should have stopped the medicine during the race. The medicine also could've caused the cramps I had on the first day. It was a revealing visit: cholesterol med ate my muscles. The race is hard enough without malicious meds. The doctor also told me he didn't think I ought to do Vol State again. I told him I didn't think *anybody* ought to do Vol State.

Entering Huntingdon, a pretty brunette was loading kids into a pickup in her yard. She looked up as I passed. "Are you crewed or screwed?" she shouted. She knew something about this race. I grasped my two chest bottles, like cylindrical mammaries. "I have to find my own water," I answered.

I remembered something useful about Huntingdon from last time. The hotel where I needed to stay was a mile south of the square. And there was no place to find food there, nothing. Last time I'd ordered a pizza from my room. This time I stopped at a restaurant just off the square called Mallard's. It was a chance to have supper before marching out to the boonies.

I was sitting eating a veggie plate. I looked up and here came Sergio with Lynda on his flank. We met again.

"How's the food?"

"The beans are good."

They joined me and ordered pasta. We talked a bit. Then I had to shove off, ever seeking solitude, it seemed.

At the Hermitage Hotel, while I was checking in, John Price, the Vol State guru, showed up in the lobby. That surprised me. I wasn't making very good time and I figured he was far ahead. The fact that he wasn't, made me feel a little better about my pace.

Hotel clerks are usually helpful. I told the lady clerk

I'd be leaving long before breakfast and asked could she find me something now that I could eat in the morning. She checked a couple cabinets and came up with two cups of yoghurt.

I was at mile sixty-eight. I was about to get a lot slower. Would my feverish legs recover? That was the question. They could get a lot worse. I knew there was only one chance. On day three, I'd have to walk the whole way and give my legs a rest, no running at all. I figured that was the only chance I had.

Chapter Three

The Benjamin Project

So, I could only walk.

I hit the street at six past three, long before daylight. It was going to be a long day because I planned to avoid running. I had to walk, give my quads a rest to see if the fever and soreness would leave them. I didn't know if that would work, but it was the best choice I had. The moon was a little lower than the previous day. In lighting my way, its light was negligible, but it's presence in the sky was a comfort somehow. I always looked for it. I walked with my little LED lighting the way in dark places.

I'd made myself a shiny bib by attaching reflective tape to an old race number. I kept it pinned on the front of my shirt for the nighttime segments. The safety pins rusted and stained my white shirt. Road grime was beginning to settle in. Even with the reflective bib, I stepped off the pavement when a car approached in front—unless it showed early signs of moving left. The driver was likely as sleepy as I was.

The only part of today's route that was shaded was the first two miles, which I covered in the dark. Then the route joined a wide four-lane, U.S. 22, headed due south. I dreaded that stretch for its unrelenting sun. When the sun first comes up, all pinkish-pale, it looks harmless and downright benign. But you learn better. It's trying to kill you. I remembered its heat cooking on my legs yesterday afternoon.

In nine miles there would be something, the little town of Clarksburg, a town with one street—and I was walking on it. A few stores, farm supply and so forth, were setting strung along the road and that's about it. But I remembered a market where I could get water and a bite to eat. By the time I got there, the sun was no longer anyone's friend.

In the market, I found Cathie and Troy Johnson, stretched out on the benches of a wall booth, cooling off and their packs sprawling on the table. They'd had enough for a while. I declined to sit and instead rushed about getting water and Gatorade from the coolers.

"There's some ice here," Cathie said pointing at the soda fountain.

"I don't want it."

"Why not?"

"I don't want to get used to it."

I was pouring the Gatorade into one of my bottles, missed the bottle, hit the floor and table. I went to clean it up, but there were no towels in the bathroom. I had to leave the mess. I apologized to the clerk, a young Indian fellow, as I checked out. I felt bad about it.

"Don't worry. It's okay. Don't worry at all," he told me, even though I'd created a chore for him.

I said my goodbyes to Cathie and Troy and marched out, eating a banana as I rejoined route 22. Next stop Parker's Crossroads, then Lexington.

Maggie Silvers was a Tennessee Tech cross-country runner I'd known a few years earlier, when she was a student at the University where I'd worked. She grew up in Lexington. As I ran this segment in 2013, she was living an apparent glamorous life, dividing her time between Aspen and Miami and other places. From wherever she was on that day, she sent a message to her dad, Tom Silvers, to go find me and make a picture. That led to a startling surprise. I was running south on the northbound shoulder of that merciless, wide four lane when suddenly a motorcycle pulled alongside, also traveling opposite the traffic. The rider was wearing a full-coverage helmet, and the voice in that bucket said, "Are you Dallas Smith?"

I stopped and he unmasked. I'd met Tom Silvers at a race once, too long ago to recognize him now. He soon told me who he was and why he'd come. I stood utterly amazed. I had no idea I'd see anybody I knew here. And I was grateful someone would want to cheer me along, especially his glamorous daughter. Of course, I posed for a photo before he cranked up and took off again. Another thought: here was a man who I'd learn was even a couple years older than I was, blasting around on a motorcycle. That's good. The incident gave me something to think about all the way to Parker's Crossroads. Then something else, equally amazing, happened, something colored by a new awareness I'd recently acquired.

A young man I've corresponded with, Dusty Wilson, is a recent industrial engineering graduate from Tennessee Tech. He runs a website called the Benjamin Project. His concept is very simple. He walks up to a total stranger and hands her or him a one-hundred-dollar bill and walks away. Recall that Benjamin Franklin's picture is on the hundred. There's absolutely no catch. He hands over the hundred and a card with the site's URL where recipients can say what they did with the gift if they want to. But they don't even have to do that.

The gift is not about helping the poor, it's not charity in that sense. The recipient is someone he picks out of a crowd that may or may not need money. How does he make money doing this? He doesn't. It's not about money. It's about generosity—his. And it's about gratitude— theirs.

This young man contacted me after reading an essay I'd written about gratitude, called *How Insensitive,* and he wanted permission to use it on his website. The incident I'd written about involved a seven-year-old-boy and it changed my life in a way that affects me yet—and would affect my actions at Parker's Crossroad. The following was my description of the lesson a little boy taught me:

> You'll likely not find a more joyous place than the fountain at Cookeville's Dogwood Park. On warm sunny days little kids by the dozens play in the water, stomping on the jets that shoot up from the surface, squealing and running

through the splash and spray from the fountain's enormous bowl overhead. Watchful parents sit on the benches and parapets and on blankets spread on the ground.

That was the scene as I jogged past this morning. I stopped on the walk and looked back to count the kids playing there. After counting two dozen I quit, although there were others nearby I could've included.

While I was standing there a little boy seven or eight years old walked up and offered me a bottle of water and a pack of Oreo cookies. I glanced down. The bottle had beads of water condensed on it. I put my hand on his shoulder to reply,

"Why, thank you! That's awful nice of you, but I'm close to home. I don't really need anything."

The little boy lowered his eyes, bowed his head, turned and walked slowly back to his family's blanket carrying his water and cookies.

Immediately, I regretted my decision. The little boy had wanted to help and I rebuffed him, took away any joy his act might have brought. I was only three miles from home. That's a small distance for a marathoner. In very truth, I didn't need anything. But I could have at least opened the offered water and poured some of it into my waist-pack bottle. And I could have said, "Open the pack of cookies and I'll share them with you."

But I didn't think quickly enough. Running

on, I was angry with my failure and brooded about it all the way home. And I made a rule so that next time I won't have to depend on quick thinking: Take an offer of food and water even if you don't need either. Anyone generous enough to share what they have with a stranger should be rewarded with the satisfaction of having helped. I'd deprived the little boy of that satisfaction and maybe robbed him of a valuable lesson of generosity toward others.

Instead, I'd given the opposite lesson: Why bother?

The little boy was shy and soft-spoken. Perhaps he'd had to work up his courage to approach the stern old jogger. His offer deserved better— from one old enough to know better.

The kindred principles of generosity and gratitude, opposite sides of the same coin, were brought home to me by the incident. The lesson makes it hard for me to refuse a gift. But if you are an unaided runner in Vol State, sometimes you must.

In the McDonald's at Parker's Crossroads, I decided to have a regular sit-down meal, the only one I'd have that day. That took a little time. I didn't know people were waiting for me. With full bottles and full stomach, I headed south on 22 again. It passes over I-40 and then there's a grassy area on the left. Two women were walking across it, angling toward me. I didn't know them. They got closer. Suddenly, I recognized Marie Threadgill, a senior runner I'd once written about. The younger woman was her daughter, Ella Wish. They knew when I should have gotten there.

"You stopped to eat lunch didn't you?" Marie said. I made what I know must have been a sheepish grin and had to admit it. We made pictures. It was good to see Marie again. I'd known her a few years but I'd not met Ella. So soon after Tom Silver's surprise visit, here I was again totally surprised. And amazed, yet again, that people cared enough to meet me.

"Are you okay? Do you need anything? Anything?" They opened the back of their SUV, revealing all sorts of drinks and supplies.

Here it gets tricky. I didn't want to lose my unaided status and Marie wasn't exactly a random stranger. And although there was no planning on my part in the meeting, if I took any help, I could be skirting what to me was disaster. I didn't want to spurn their offer, but I also didn't want to lose my unaided status. Fortunately, I had an alibi.

"No, thanks so much. I'm in good shape. I just ate and filled up my bottles too, so I don't need anything." I was in the clear, standing there in the burning sun, going straight. Then—

"How about some sun screen? You need any sunscreen?"

Ah, suddenly a notion. "Okay, I can put on some sunscreen."

Marie handed me the tube and watched as I smeared the stuff on my bony arms and neck. So, I let them help, after all, and thanked them profusely. I took their help—

they thought—but, in fact I'd put sunscreen on that morning, as I always did. And I had a bottle in my pack. I could stop and reapply it whenever I wanted to.

I accepted help and I didn't accept help—because I didn't need the lotion and it didn't aid me in finishing the race. I think the spirit of "screwed" runners understand. My conscious is clear. A friend helped me. I let her help, and thereby helped her. Surely I won't be punished for being a friend doing a good deed.

Those events happened two years ago, and they came to mind as I approached the McDonald's again. This time, Ella met me at the restaurant. I was standing outside eating a sausage and biscuit, when I heard, "Hello, Dallas." Ella had driven up just behind me. I asked about Marie, why she hadn't come.

"She's out riding her bicycle," was Ella's answer.

Figures, she stays in shape. I hated missing her. But it was good to visit with Ella at least.

The sun was burning full-bore in my face now, as I headed toward Lexington, on a wide highway without a hint of shade. This was likely the third day now where the mercury hit triple digits. I can't say for sure because I made it a point to disrespect it by not checking it. Give no quarter. I was moving slowly because of my poisoned quads. I didn't know if they'd recover or just get worse. Cathie and Troy had passed me in a brisk march and gone on out of sight.

Going into Lexington, I had my head down to shade out the sun and wasn't paying attention. When I looked up a figure was coming toward me on the walk. It was

Marie. She'd finished her ride and come looking for me. I got a hug out of that.

"Where can I get a copy of your last book?" she asked.

"Easiest thing is to order it from Amazon."

"But I want you to sign it."

"Shoot, if I had my car, I could give you one."

After all, she was the inspiration for part of it. We left the problem unsolved. But I didn't forget it. A few weeks later, after I arrived back home, I sent Ella a private message asking for Marie's street address. Ella guessed why and said she'd not tell Marie. I wrote a note in the book and sent it to Marie. Imagine her surprise. In return, she sent me a sweet thank you note. Gratitude, thanks enough.

At Lexington the course turns abruptly east, the direction we must eventually go. That would be good, after facing south into the sun for nearly three days, at least we get cooked on a different side. There's a market at the turn. I went in to fill my bottles and get a bite to eat. It was midday. Troy Johnson came in. He and Cathie had put up in a hotel across the street. They were going to sleep while it was hot and head east at night when it was cooler. The plan made sense. He left the store with a bag full of food and drinks. I left the store and headed east.

The hours wore on. The sun hissed and sizzled on the back of my neck. I was going pitifully slow on my mangled legs. Troy's plan was making more sense.

There is a store building abandoned from a past era. It sits close to the road and has a covered concrete porch around which weeds grow. I remembered it from last time and I found it again. I used my pack for a pillow. The cool concrete felt good on my back and I went to sleep.

It was only a nap. I got up after fifteen minutes and re-entered the scalding bath of sunshine, trudging east, the sun behind me bearing down hard.

I didn't well know where I was, where along that east-running road I was, how much further it was to Parsons. Side roads I saw I couldn't find named on my map. When you don't know where you are, there can be no sense of progress. Then, finally, I came to a road teeing into U.S 412 and State Route 20, the road I was traveling on. That intersection precisely told me my location. I'd only come seven miles since Lexington. I had used three hours to cover seven miles. I stood looking at my map in utter and flabbergasted astonishment. How could I go that slow, how was it possible? Of course it included the nap, but that wasn't long. Seven miles in three hours was even slower than my normal walk.

Standing alone on the roadside in the burning sun, the realization came down hard. I had meant to go slow, true. I had meant to walk to let my quads heal, true. Now, I had a new definition of what "slow" really meant. My legs were compromised more than I'd known. Of course, it was after the race that I discovered the cholesterol medicine I took each night was eating my muscles.

At least there was a market. I went in and replenished my water and Gatorade. Since my muscles cramps on the first day, I'd made a practice of drinking as much Gatorade as water, so as to replenish electrolytes. I found a picnic table outside in the shade on the market's east end.

Soon a Harley-Davidson Motorcycle couple joined

me, the typical couple you see nowadays—well fed and old enough to have the time and money to ride around the country, and yet young enough to still do it. The woman took the seat across the table from me, the man a lawn chair nearby. She had jet black hair, which likely wasn't so naturally dark. I beat them to the punch.

"Ya'll doing all right?"

"We're just riding around. It's hot, ain't it?"

"Yes, it is. I figured it'd be a little cooler on that motor-cycle, with the air..."

"That helps, but the helmets are hot. It's just hot."

"Where all have ya'll been?"

They described a round trip up in Missouri, the wom-an doing most of the talking, the man chiming in occasion-ally. They were nearly home now, a place nearby I didn't recognize, probably why they knew about this market.

"What are you doing?" she asked.

"Oh, I'm just cooling off right now. And resting. I've been on the road."

She looked at my bottles. You riding a bicycle or sumpin'?"

"I'm running, except I'm walking today because I hurt my legs."

"Running? Couldn't you find a cooler time to run, like after the sun sets or sumpin'?"

"I'm in a race. And I'm losing."

"A race..? Where is it? Is it like a marathon or sump-in'?"

"It normally starts at Dorena Landing in Missouri. This year the river was so high the ferry couldn't operate. We couldn't get to Missouri so we started in Hickman, Kentucky. And it ends on top of Sand Mountain in Georgia."

"Can you just stop anytime you want to?"

"I can. But the clock never stops. 'The road goes on forever and the clock never stops,' is my saying."

"How far is it?"

"It's called the Vol State 500k. 500k is about 314 miles. Yeah, it's a long haul."

I was describing a foreign world they'd never heard of.

"Well, that's the...That heads all. I never heard of anything like that, that people do that."

"Not many do. Just a handful."

"Why do you want to do it?"

"I don't know. Maybe if I knew, I wouldn't do it. Maybe I do it to find out."

It was time to put the sun on my neck again. I wanted to get to Parsons before milk time. Not that I'd be milking cows, but if I was late getting in the sack, I'd be late getting up next morning, which would make me late reaching the next day's goal, and so on, a downward spiral growing steeper and steeper.

I had a new definition of slow. I could see why runners get in trouble and sink deeper and deeper until only hopelessness is left. On the Google update map they show numbers for the runners strung out along the course. Marching behind them is another icon. It looks like death in a robe carrying a scythe, and it moves forward at a pace of 31.4 miles each day, the minimum speed required to finish in ten days. If he's on your heels, you're in trouble.

A friend, Diane Taylor, who has finished this race three times, dropped out just last year. "I could see where I needed to get to, but I just couldn't get there," she told me before this race started. I was learning. Forget all the rules. This race rips the heart out of running.

Soon, above the rolling road ahead, I could see buildings of a town, still a mile or more away. As I got closer a young man was standing in his yard, looking on. He yelled, "You need any water or anything?" I didn't but I walked across his yard to talk. That's how I am.

"I know what ya'll are doing," he said. "I think it's amazing. Are you okay, do you need anything at all? I like to help. I've seen some others go by."

"Actually, I'm stopping in Parsons. So I'm fine. I'll have food and water there. I'm okay, just looking forward to stopping."

"I think it's great, what you're doing. I can't imagine…One day I'm going to try it. If you don't mind, how old are you?"

"I'm seventy-five. If I can finish, I'll be the oldest to have ever run it unsupported."

"I was going to ask that," he said. "I bet you make it. I'm going to look for you on the Google update. What's your name?"

I told him and he said it a few times, rolling his eyes up to make a memory picture.

"We've been in Panama City on vacation," he said. "We just got back today. I saw some runners go by. I'm catching up. I gotta mow my yard."

I glanced around at the scattered shade trees, the neatly cut—I thought—grass. "Your yard looks better un-mowed than mind does mowed," I said.

"Well, I like to keep it neat."

I left the friendly man and drifted on. The Parsons Inn appeared to be a 1950s era hotel, an office building and two low buildings of rooms in the back. It was better than a store porch. Once I got to the room, I noted the time, 7:46 p.m. I'd started in Huntingdon at 3:06 a.m. and so spent nearly seventeen hours on the road. I had come thirty-nine miles without any running. It had been a brutal day of hot sun on broad highways that offered no shade, just what I'd signed up for.

According to my map, the hotel sat near the 107-mile mark. So, I was about a third of the way to the rock ledge in Georgia, after two and a half days. Officially, the three-day mark didn't come until seven-thirty the next morning. I knew I'd be a few more miles down the road by then.

My hotel routine is set. The first thing is a bath, after being hot and sweaty all day. I follow John Price's advice on how I do it. I step into the shower with my running clothes on, and rinse them at the same time I take a bath. I wrap the wet shorts, socks and shirt in a towel to draw some of the water out and after a while I hang them up to dry. I sleep in the raw while my clothes dry. Usually, they don't get completely dry by the time I put them back on, but it makes little difference. They would get wet with sweat soon, anyway.

This night, there was no restaurant near the hotel, so I sat wrapped in a towel and ate in the room. The little market where I stopped just before the hotel didn't have any Beanee Weenees. I ate a can of cold chili instead, plus some peanut butter crackers and a candy bar.

Breakfast in the mornings varies. I shoot for pastry, juice or fruit and milk. I'll have coffee if the room has a coffee-maker. But I substitute and depart from dogma. You have to be flexible. What I can find where I am, is what I eat.

Despite the extraordinarily friendly man I'd just met, Parsons is the locale of an act of inhuman barbarity, unbounded evil. Twenty-year-old nursing student, Holly Bobo, was abducted and killed in 2011. Two years ago, when I ran through here, the crime had not been solved. The hotel office had handbills showing her picture and asking for information. I remember looking at the picture of the smiling young woman.

At that point they'd not even found her body. Her skull was found just this past September. This May, two months before Vol State started, three men were indicted for aggravated kidnapping and murder. A month ago, in June, the special prosecutor announced that she'd seek the death penalty if they were convicted.

Clearly, evil is somewhere about and maybe even nearby, on the country roads and in the streets of the towns we run through. Holly Bobo's tragic case illustrates that. I knew I'd be running the main street of Parsons in the dark the next morning. Yet, I carried no weapon, not even pepper spray. I doubt any runner carried a gun. Keeping up with and carrying the weight of a pistol would complicate the run. It was prohibitive in my judgment—even if you wanted to carry one. But I have other reasons.

I grew up with a gun in my hand. I must have been no more than nine when my parents gave me a single-shot .410. Thereafter, I'd hang out in the hills, hunting squirrels and shooting the varmints that ate our crops, the crows and groundhogs. My dad was a trick shooter and the best marksman in the community, which in that era was an important skill. I picked up some of his skills. Hand me a gun and I knew instinctively how to safely handle it. Soon I was accurate enough to kill a mess of squirrels with my dad's Smith and Wesson .22 revolver.

In my freshman year at Tennessee Tech, I tried out for the rifle team. I ended up being the runner-up high scorer that year. In my second year, I was the high scorer and team MVP. Rifle competition was a varsity sport and intercollegiate competition was sanctioned by the National Rifle Association then. In my fourth year, I ranked sixteenth nationally. In 1980, rifle was sanctioned by NCAA. My old team won three consecutive national championships, the only NCAA national championship of any kind ever won by Tennessee Tech.

I own over two dozen guns now, sporting and hunting guns mostly, shotguns and .22-caliber rifles. There's not a single "black" gun in my collection, the military-style weapons that have flooded the country in the last twenty years. Those weapons hold no interest for me. They're machines of war. My guns are locked in a safe that's bolted to the floor back home, where they should be.

All this is to say I know something about guns, yet I don't carry one. I hold a permit to carry a gun, yet I don't carry one. I don't carry a gun for the same reason I don't buy lottery tickets: I know arithmetic. There are two compounding improbabilities: The probability I'll need to protect myself is small. Further, even if I did need to, the probability my gun would help is equally small. Because a crook knows what he's going to do and I don't. He'd have the drop on me—unless I meet every stranger that comes along with wary and fearful suspicion and with gun in hand, ever on guard. That's no way to live in civilized society.

That's the rational approach of an engineer. Decisions to carry a gun, however, aren't based on reason; they're based on emotion and fear. On that score, I'm just not afraid. So, no, I don't carry a gun. Nor do I need to. What I've met on this journey are not inimical actors bent on harm, but instead friendly people we call Road Angels.

Road Angels are the random strangers who offer runners water and food and other help. I'd encountered a surprising number already. On the night of this third day on the road in Parsons, Tennessee, it's well to remember such a hopeful and life-affirming fact.

My last chore before hitting the sack was to post some pictures and a brief narrative of the day on Facebook. The post ended on this positive note: "During that darkest of trudges, numerous Road Angels offered both cold goodies and simple human kindness. That helped."

Chapter Four

The Knife Comes Out

It was eerie quiet in Parsons. I hit U.S. 412 at 4:14 a.m. I'd slept later than usual. I drifted along Main Street, which is 412, passing dimly lighted store fronts and shops. Their muted light lent a ghostly glow to the street. Sunday morning, everyone was still asleep.

What looked like a pit bull mix was nosing around ahead, across the street on the right. He could be a problem, I thought. I had no weapon to bring against him, of course, not even a stick. I watched him. When I got nearly even, he lifted his head and gazed at me with mild curiosity a moment. Then he went back to sniffing a trash barrel. He was not on his home turf and he had no need to defend a random street location from a sleepy runner. As I traveled on, I looked back a time or two to make sure he didn't try a flanking maneuver and come circling in behind me. It worked out. We parted in peace.

This town made a lingering memory. Maybe it was because I was going through it on Sunday morning when all activities were at a halt. Despite the wide news coverage of the Holly Bobo murder here, a savage and tragic crime story, there seemed a peacefulness to the town that made it stand out to me in a way the other towns didn't.

For example, the last time I went through here, I heard what is the signature night sound of Tennessee, and especially of the Vol State night runners—katydids. Departing on the western edge of town, the trees seemed to close in a bit and suddenly I heard the familiar keening. The insects don't register as loud to me as they once did. I can hear their high-frequency call with only my left ear. Their sound can be all around me, but no matter which way I face, they always seem to be on my left. Owing to my ear's frequency response, the sound is somewhat modified, as well, an almost individually pronounced *skr–i-i-i-tch, skr-i-i-i-tch, skr-i-i-i-tch, skritccch-et!* It's not the same singing drone a person of normal hearing would hear, or the same sound I heard as a young man. It's the aural equivalent of looking at purple and seeing only the red, receiving only half the information in the wave front. But yet, even though modified, katydids still make a pleasing night sound to me.

I heard an owl. It made one plaintive call *whooo* and then shushed, as if the ripple of its own voice ruptured the night stillness and somehow frightened it into silence. Just that one sad, mournful call, a single, plaintive musical syllable, it came to me soft through the dawning, and I waited but heard no other greeting. Lonely though he sounded, he was no more lonesome than I. I carried his soft call on into that cloudy day. I carry it still, one of those indelible memories of a place you'd never expect yet somehow gain.

At the location where I heard the owl, what I noticed this time were the frogs. There seemed to be several different kinds, including one that made a call almost like barking, a frog sound I'd not heard before. And of course in that mix a bullfrog was grunting. It was badly outnumbered.

The most special sound, and a sound I had not heard at all in many years, until I ran Vol State, was a whip-poor-will. That sound evokes nostalgia for the countryside like no other. When I was a boy, I used to hear one at milking time, in the hackberry tree on the hill above the barn. Now, as I left Parsons, one in the trees sang his forlorn call.

How important are animals? Important enough that the impressions and memories I have of a town are dominated by the animals of its environs—the frogs and birds. Although it was yet dark and cool, their hopeful songs would launch me into another burning day.

The moon was a stingy mistress withholding her light. She hung in the eastern sky, a slender sliver like a rueful thin smile. Each day she fell a little closer to her master the rising sun. Now the sky was beginning to lighten. A thin cool mist lay in the vale of a fallow field.

Vol State has added a new term to the running lexicon, "2 mph," a speed ordinary runners don't consider, but every Vol Stater knows. When you have no play left except a feeble walk, then that's the play you make.

You can endure even that and emerge running the next day. I did. The fever in my quads had broken overnight during a deep sleep untroubled by dreams or trips to the bathroom. Sleep and rest was the key. My injured legs no longer felt hot to the touch. I permitted myself a little running. The legs had recovered from the fever, but they weren't strong. If I ran much, the effort exhausted me. I went east into the day mixing a little running in with the walking. I would have to see how it finally played out.

I reached the Tennessee River before the seven-thirty check-in mark that officially ended day three. The river is a milestone of obvious significance. It's a crossing, after all. It cuts away the journey behind you and sets a new starting line.

The sun was just rising and I stopped for a picture. It had just cleared the distant blue ridges, the sky was reflecting bright on the river and the parapet of the bridge I stood on stretched away to the east. In that moment, a boater, likely a bass fisherman, raced south, drawing a perfect, sharp V on the serene water. It remains an endearing image. I was trotting the fog line east toward The Rock, the Tennessee River rolled north toward Kentucky and the fisherman drew an arrow south, each finding his destiny.

Four miles later, I texted Carl Laniak my position, an ebullient message maybe expressing more optimism than my condition warranted: "Dallas Smith has crossed river. Fever in quads broke. I can run. MM 117." Carl answered back: "Woohoo."

Don Winkley was not far behind me. I knew that because his crewman had parked his white van on the roadside to wait for him. We chatted, but I never learned his name. I call him "Crew." I'd pass him parked, and then a few minutes later he'd pass me and park again, after he'd met Don. One of those times we were talking, and he told me about a chalk message he'd seen on the road. "It said 'Hi, Dallas,'" he told me. I had not seen it. At first the message seemed odd. A message to me, in this distant place. But I figured it out.

I'd seen Diane Bolton passing in a car as she was crewing for someone. I was sure she'd written the message. We two share an incident here, one I refer to as "poor dallas." She and her crewman Phil Min had caught up with me at the river two years ago. Phil made some pictures of Diane and me side-by-side on the road. For two or three miles we were mostly together, back and forth. It came time for her to make her day-three call-in. I'd already texted my position. I dropped back while she talked to race director Lazarus Lake on the phone. We know what was said in that conversation because Laz wrote the transcript of it and others in an e-mail to the Vol State e-mail user group. This is Laz's hilarious account:

> this morning's check-ins are off to a flying start.
> i am groggy when the phone rings,
> after having been up most of the night waiting
> on the stinky feet
> to finally choose the correct roads into alabama
> and georgia.
>
> the connection seems to be no clearer on the
> opposite end.
>
> shaking out cobwebs, i answer;

71

"good morning! 3-day check-in"
"this is marcia"
(ah, this one remembered to tell me who was
calling!)
"so how was your night?"
"yes, yes it was."
then she hangs up.
i have all the critical information,
except where she is.

 i don't have long to think about this,
because the phone rings again.
"good morning! 3-day check-in"
"do you have any coffee?"
"no, i don't have any coffee here."
"i thought you might bring some coffee."
"no, i won't be bringing any coffee."
"oh well; i am at the church of latter day saints."
"who is i?"
"diane bolton."
"i don't know the distance for that church."
"between parsons and linden."
(that would be between 103 and 125)
"which side of the tennessee river are you on?"
"yes."
"you haven't reached the tennessee river yet?"
"oh no, we crossed that a long time ago...

but we haven't got to linden yet."
i am trying to think of a way to narrow this

down some, and she volunteers a clue.
"dallas is right behind us."
"oh, dallas."
"dallas smith. poor dallas."
"poor dallas?"
"i have a crew, and he doesn't.
(she laughs)
i think i have lost my humanity.
i should feel guilty, up here eating ice chips....

and there is poor dallas.
he doesn't have a crew.
he doesn't have anything."
then she laughs again and hangs up.

so far i know that marcia had a night,
and diane has ice chips, but would like coffee.
(also dallas still has no crew, but that is only
hear-say)

the phone rings again.
"good morning! 3-day check-in."
"this is (garbled) bruce's crew"
"and how are yall doing this morning?"
"we are doing good. bruce is at 102."
"102? it seems more likely he is at 202?"
"oh, yes. it is probably 202. not that it makes any
difference....

well, it might make a difference to bruce."

(i am sure it makes a difference to bruce.)
"i have you down, ya'll have a fun day out there."
"ok"
she hangs up.

i am not sure the vol-state is good for brain function.
but the important thing is,
everyone seemed to be in very good spirits.

i better get these results to carl,
so we can start figuring out where people are
(within a planet)

laz

This year, Diane wasn't running. She was crewing, but she remembers, as I do, that call-in. I was confident she'd written the chalk message. I wish I'd seen it.

I trudged along, some running, mostly walking. Entering the fourth day, problems were beginning to emerge, nothing serious yet, but an indication of coming attractions if I were not careful. My shoe was rubbing the top of my big toe on my left foot and the brief in my shorts was chafing my thighs. The high temperatures contribute to such problems, making everything wet with sweat. I didn't address the toe problem, because the shoes were the same model and brand that I'd worn two years earlier with only superficial blister problems. I trusted the shoes. My feet are hardened to running. I usually don't have blister problems. I figured my feet would be okay. That figuring would turn out to be horribly wrong.

The chafing problem caused more distress now. Each morning I'd apply Body Glide to diminish friction. I also lowered the shorts a couple inches so they could rub a new place and let the old place rest. That improved my style category and gave me a hip-hop vibe, trotting down the road in drooping britches. But it didn't completely stop the chafing. I would have to look for a different solution.

I remembered a guy two years earlier who had the same problem, but a different body part. He wrapped his scrotum with duct tape. Which seemed an imperfect solution. That's the fate of the unsupported runner—making do with what he has or he can find.

I had two problems I'd need to watch and eventually to address. This country boy always carries a penknife. It was one of just three items in my emergency repair kit. The other two were a piece of shoe string and four safety pins. You may need to tie something and you may need to pin something. Plus you can drain a blister with a safety pin. My toe and chafing problem would eventually require the knife.

Today's road, a two-lane, was a pleasant change from the wide four-lanes of the last two days. The route ran up a valley, climbed a hill and descended the other side into Linden, a place I remember for a market one sees upon first entering town. I was looking for it.

I went into K-M market, bought some Beanee Weenees, peanuts and milk. Three booths line the distant wall opposite check-out. I walked back there and saw a pack resting on one of the benches.

Hmm, there's a runner around here somewhere.

I sat down and started eating.

Jameelah emerged from the restroom. She was the runner who, along with me, had been saved by the good ole boys in the transmission shop on the very first day and the runner whose name I'd mispronounced as Camilla all that day. She'd slept on the ground somewhere near the river the previous night, she told me. We were together again.

She showed me her foot. "What would you do?" she asked.

A big blister had formed on the ball. She had a cotton pad and tape over it. Blisters form from friction at pressure points. It seemed to me that the pad would only increase the pressure. The tape would soon come loose in the sweaty shoe.

"I guess I'd leave the bandage off and put Body Glide on it and go on."

It was advice I'd eventually have to give myself. Some runners carry elaborate blister repair kits. I was not such a runner. I was discouraged for her, that she had such a blister so early in the run.

She didn't appear to know what Body Glide was. I showed her mine and told her she was welcome to use it. She took my advice and smeared some of the lubricant on the blister. She finished charging her phone, and I finished eating, and we left the store together, drifting through Linden like two homeless specters.

First thing, I apologized for mispronouncing her

name.

"I realized it when I saw 'Jameelah' on the race up-date. I knew I'd been saying the wrong name. I'm really sorry."

She dismissed the incident. "It's all right," she said.

She needed help for the blister problem. "Before Body Glide came along, runners used Vaseline," I told her as we walked along. "The advantage of Vaseline is that you can get it anywhere." Any market would have Vaseline, and she was going to need it.

On the other end of town we came to the Chamber of Commerce. It was a small frame building that looked more like a lakeside cabin than a city building. We stopped in to refill our bottles. They had prepared a welcome for run-ners. It was a surprise.

The solicitous caretaker, a slender middle-aged wom-an said, "Come back here!"

I walked to the table. A cardboard box was filled with snacks.

"Take as much as you want!"

I knew the enthusiastic woman would be disappoint-ed if I didn't take something, so I picked out a granola bar. Jameelah and I continued on.

Shortly, there came a wide intersection, a market sit-ting on the opposite side. It was just before the road cross-es the Buffalo River and leaves town. Jameelah angled off toward the market. I guessed she was going to buy some Vaseline—she needed it. I was unsure whether to follow or go on. My hesitation showed my indecision.

Looking back, she said, "Go on. I'll catch up."

She might, but I didn't expect it. I felt bad about her blister.

So, I went on. I had my own rat killing to do, as the man said. I drifted across the Buffalo. It looked like a nice river. You could probably catch fish on a float trip or by wading. I headed up the long hill, leaving Linden and the Buffalo behind. Half way up the hill I looked back and saw a white cap in the distance.

Don Winkley was going to catch me.

Couple miles later he did. I hadn't wasted much time, even running a little. The road forked—U.S. 100 split left from 20 and 412—and a market sat at the intersection. I needed water again. I made the right turn and started to go to the store, but Don was closing quickly. He was moving briskly in something not quite a walk not quite a run, but more like some combination. It's what good ultrarunners do. I stood and waited.

"I was going to go to the market, but I thought I'd stay on the road and let you officially pass me before I do," I told him.

Roads follow valleys and then they climb hills. This one did. It went up and up and up a valley that grew ever more narrow. I needed water. I walked toward a house where someone was working on a RV in the back yard. Then I saw a Confederate flag hanging on a yard pole and did a U-turn. I got water a little later at a home where I remember stopping two years earlier. The man remembered me, too. I was going to fill up at a faucet I remembered in the yard. The man insisted I come in and get a couple bottles of cold water, kindness like I'd met all along the way.

Further on, a private picnic shelter stood near the road. I stretched out on the concrete and took a brief nap. When I headed on, I passed Don and Crew taking a nap on the grass under a platform in a field. The thought *chiggers!* hit me. As a practice and a hedge against that particular irritating pest, I'd put on DEET each morning, just as I did sunscreen. Small price to pay to avoid even one infuriating chigger bite.

No chigger bites yet, but as the day wore on, physical problems mounted. My shorts were still chafing the inside of my thighs, even though I was wearing them drooping low and using Body Glide too. I analyzed the chafing mechanism closer and came to a conclusion: The bulge my scrotum made in the shorts brief was the rubbing culprit. I knew I had to resort to the knife sooner or later.

Ultrarunner and triathlete Kay Scott had added me as a Facebook friend a few months earlier. I'd never seen her or met her. There are lots of runners like that, who are friends on social media who I don't really know, aside from their posts. Their posts tell me a lot, though.

I'd finished the last bottle of cold water I got at the remembered house, and I'd been carrying the empty bottle. I like my hands free and I didn't know what to do with the bottle. Sometimes, I'd crush them and force them into my little pack, but that wasn't a satisfying solution. I came to a wide spot on the grassy shoulder where the rural mail carrier pulls off to put mail in the box standing at the edge. There was my solution. I stepped over and set the bottle on the ground against the post. I felt like if the homeowner knew my situation, he wouldn't mind picking it up for me.

Just then, I got busted in the act. A white car pulled up and stopped. A young woman got out, leaving her five-or-so-year-old daughter in the car.

"I'm Kay Scott," she said. Ah, a friend. "You look strong," she said. That was a kindness.

"You caught me standing. I just left that empty bottle, figuring the owner wouldn't mind."

"Oh, I can take some trash." She fetched the bottle and pitched it in her car. She'd been visiting in Tennessee, she told me, and was on her way back home to Texas. She should have been blasting west on I-40, not over on this two-lane. It's a hard all-day drive.

"You mean you're on your way back to Dallas and you took a detour just to see some runners?"

"How could I not?"

Endurance is her sport and she wanted to see the crazy Vol State runners. You can count Kay as another Road Angel. But she had to rush off. Her car was partially blocking a lane, traffic was passing and her little girl had gotten out. It was dangerous. Her stop was a pleasant distraction for a moment. And this run is comprised of many such moments, stacked one upon another all the way to the end of the day.

I remembered that there was a Mexican restaurant a block from the hotel in Hohenwald. I'd been looking forward to it all day. It would be wonderful if I could sit down for a real meal and beer. I climbed the hill out of the valley thinking about it. "Soon you'll climb the hill and then it's a short ways to town," Kay had said. A short ways in a car may not seem so short on foot.

I was a mule smelling the barn. Going into town, I started running. I was running pretty well too, enough so that a woman passing in an Explorer gave me a woo-hoo yell. Or something like that. The eatery was called Rio Colorado, and I passed it just before reaching the hotel.

I saw another runner at the hotel in the lobby. She told me she had quit. But then she had un-quit and decided to go on as a crewed runner. That is an option, if someone you know has a crew they can share with you, or if you know someone you can call to come out and crew for you. Later race results showed she quit still again, the next day.

In my room, I took a shower and washed my clothes. I carry an extra pair of shorts but not an extra shirt. I donned my windbreaker instead. Even though anxious to eat, I decided to compose a blog post first. Varying my routine like that was stupid. The results were that I reached Rio Colorado at precisely 8:00 p.m., their closing time. The kind woman seated me anyway. Just as my beer and burrito came, the meal I'd looked forward to all day, my phone rang, the only call I had in the whole journey.

It was Josh Hite, my running buddy back in Cookeville. He'd been following my progress and called to see how I was doing. Despite the supper delay, the call was helpful. I told him how the brief in my shorts were chafing my thighs and how I thought I'd have to use my knife. He agreed. It was time for the knife. Decision made. I finished supper and went back to the hotel. This country boy had a penknife in his pack, necessary equipment. I keep it sharp.

The knife is made in the U.S.A. by Bear and Sons, in

Jacksonville, Alabama. It has second-cut stag handles and stainless steel blades. It's not as pretty or as expensive as a Case, also made in this country, but the metal is good and I keep a keen edge on it. Now it came out. I dreaded using it. I debated putting it off one more day. But, no, it was time.

I stabbed the clip blade through the top of my sneaker, right at the place where for a couple of days now it had been pressing on my big toe. I extended the cut in two directions, toward the front of the shoe and backwards, leaving an inch-and-a-half split over where my big toenail rested. That would take the pressure off.

For the chafing problem, I was going to find out if free flopping was better than firm rubbing. I made two cuts across the briefs in my shorts, removing the bottom section altogether, leaving a flap hanging down inside at the front and back. I hated mutilating a good pair of shorts, but I wasn't going to duct-tape any body parts. Now, I was going to be barely decent, or to say it another way, I was going to be nearly indecent. I hoped no one but me would know.

I was at mile 145. I had come just thirty-eight miles for the day. Day four would not end until seven-thirty next morning. If I could get myself twelve miles down the road before then, I'd be at mile 157, which is halfway. Halfway in four days, it was a goal I wanted to shoot for.

Chapter Five

Circling the Tire Store

Hohenwald was not yet awake when I made my three a.m. departure. I made the town mine and left part of my shorts there. Then I sneaked out like a thief in the middle of the night. Columbia was my next target.

I wasn't looking forward to it. A long stretch was not only a big wide sun-washed highway, it was under construction to boot. By leaving at three I'd have four and a half hours before the day-four check-in and I hoped, even with stops and chores, that that would let me gain the twelve miles I needed to be at the halfway point of 157 miles in four days.

Still again, my stingy mistress hung barely above the horizon, heralding the sunrise, smiling thinly down as I headed into pre-dawn. I guessed this would be the last morning I'd see the moon. Well, so long. It's been nice.

After daylight I began looking for a place I thought I'd remember. There was no specific landmark, rather a vague image in my mind: the road would be descending and curving gently to the right and there'd be a guardrail on the left, and at the far end of the guardrail there would be a crash absorber structure. Beyond there would be pasture land. It was something to look for.

The crash absorber is a bulbous structure at the end of the guardrail that's flat on top, a table for my pack. Two years ago I'd laid my pack on it to dig out my sunglasses. I noticed a black garbage bag sprawling open underneath the rail. Pornographic magazines and videos were spilling out. I nudged a DVD to get a better look. It showed a couple of young blond-headed women in, let's say, provocative clothes. The title made a disingenuous literary reference, something like, *A City of Two Tails*. It was that sort of invention, not terribly subtle or witty.

But then pornographers aren't noted for subtle wit. Why did I happen to stop precisely where the bag was? Divine intervention, my humble pace combined with the magic timing of daylight. Why was the bag even there at all? Did some guy throw away his whole collection, afraid his wife would find it? Maybe his wife *did* find it. Maybe *she* threw it away. Maybe it was the castoff proceeds of the divorce settlement. Why on the roadside and not the dumpster? I have no answers. Only questions. A novelist would go off on a whole long riff. Me? I just trotted on down the road.

Now I trotted by that place again, and I thought I recognized it as the right place. I didn't expect the bag to still be there after two years, but you can't help looking. All clear.

The Natchez Trace Parkway crosses U.S. 412, my

route. There was a new bridge overhead with graceful curves. I ran under it remembering something someone said on the bus. I wish I'd listened better—something about rangers setting out some food and drinks. That would be important to know right now. I was facing a fairly long stretch where water could be a problem. Last time here I'd gotten water from a construction foreman who had a cooler bolted to his pickup. Construction was still going on but I couldn't depend on finding that guy again.

The sign ahead was advertising a campground and I could see a small building back off the road that appeared to be the campground office. It was worth a try. I made my way along the gravel drive. Sure enough, on little more than a hunch, I found a cooler of drinks at the front of the building. I sat and had a Coke and some crackers and refilled my bottles. I didn't see a collection box so I put a ten dollar bill in the tray of the cooler. There was a maroon van sitting in the parking lot. If it wasn't Jan's meat wagon, it was its twin sister. Jan was probably in there asleep. I wasn't about to mess with the meat wagon. Get me away from here. On up the road I continued, if not fat, dumb and happy, I was at least loaded with water.

There was an odd sensation I had when last I ran through here: I felt like I was in Arkansas. How one gets in an Arkansas state of mind, I'm not sure. Just something about the rolling woodlands that resembled a scene I'd seen and even forgotten long ago in Arkansas maybe. Construction of the four-lane was still going on just as it had been two years earlier. I watched the minutes roll toward my check-in time. I wanted to be at mile 157 by then.

Trouble was the signs of side roads were down due to the construction. It was hard to know precisely where I was. Big Swan Creek comes at mile 155. I remembered it from two years ago. I needed to be two miles beyond that steam at seven-thirty if I was to make my goal.

Finally, I decided I must be there, or at least close enough for government work, as the old saying goes. I rested my pack on top of a red and white construction barrel and made a picture. The ensemble looked like the hillbilly cousin of R2D2. Then I sent Carl Laniak a text: "Dallas Smith at 157."

My left big toe felt much better now, since I'd done the surgery on my shoe. It had been an annoyance that I tolerated too long. If you do endurance sports you learn to ignore aggravation. That's not always a good thing. More troublesome than the toe were the bottoms of my feet and toes. The heat I felt in them told me blisters were forming. The balls of my feet were on their way to looking like Jameelah's. Maybe they already were. I didn't stop to inspect the damage. Out of sight, out of mind, was my approach.

There was an aspect of the accumulating foot damage I understood much better than my lack of urgency showed. Walking, which I was doing to a much greater extent than I'd planned, will blister your feet, even though they may be hardened to running. My friend David Wingard of South Carolina illustrated that fact to me in this race two years ago. He's a veteran long-distance runner and was not worried about blister problems in Vol State. He was using the race as training for walking the Appalachian Trail. Accordingly, even though he was accustomed to running, he walked the whole way. That didn't go well.

On the second day, I saw him at the hotel where we both stayed. He came gingerly walking barefooted along the sidewalk.

"You're limping," I said.

"Yep, I blistered up."

He went on to tell me what he'd learned, that walking will blister a runner's feet where running wouldn't. It was a revelation to him. And he was disappointed he'd not realized that before.

"Who knew?" he said with resignation, as if to say any runner ought to know it. In fact, not many do.

David's lesson was not my lesson, it seemed, or at least it didn't appear to be. I was in the process of learning it again. My leg weakness forced me to walk more than I'd planned. And my feet were falling to the same injury David had discovered. I knew what was happening, but I didn't stop and remove my shoes to inspect the damage. I could feel it well enough. I knew. Besides, what could I do? I carried no blister repair kit.

The root of my trouble extended all the way back to a little pill I was innocently taking every night for high cholesterol. It was destroying my leg muscles and forcing me to walk. And now the walking was leading to foot problems. On the road I couldn't know about the little pill's quiet evil. Not until after the race, when my doctor ran the blood test, did I realize the true enormity of what the pill had done.

Foot problems aside, I have to focus on the road. Even a new four-lane follows the valley and then climbs a hill. Then this one changed to the original two-lane going down the other side. Trees hung over it, bringing relief from the sun. It seemed such a change that I stopped and made a picture that showed nothing more than a mere shaded lane.

Hampshire is a sleepy little community between Hohenwald and Columbia. As I entered, a woman stopped her car and sat talking to me. She was hauling three kids of various ages. She wanted to know what I was doing. She had seen another runner or two. Her car and I occupied the middle of the road. I looked anxiously up and down.

"Don't worry, nobody'll run over you. I live here. These drivers won't hurt you."

Well, maybe, but what if a driver that doesn't live here comes blasting through? She was my welcome to Hampshire. The conversation was a welcome rest. We could have talked a long time had we not been in the middle of the road. She finally released me.

There is a woman named Linda who works in the Whiteside Market. She makes the best baloney sandwich between here and The Rock and places beyond, one piled high with meat, lettuce and tomatoes. I wanted one of those sandwiches. She still worked there. I found her behind the counter. I asked her to make me a sandwich like I remembered. I sat at a table with the sandwich, a can of Beanee Weenees and a bottle of milk, enjoying lunch, when the first runner I'd seen all day walked through the door. It was my old friend Sergio. I hadn't seen him since the second day, at Mallard's restaurant in Huntingdon.

"What did you do with Lynda?" I asked him.

"She wanted to stop at Wal-Mart and buy a dress."

Did he say that? I believe he did. Maybe she got tired of wearing britches. I didn't know. I felt like he was going to wait here for her to catch up. He'd stayed the night, like me, in Hohenwald. "

"What time did you leave Hohenwald?" I wondered.

"Seven o'clock," he said.

"Seven o'clock!" I yelled. "I left at three, and you got here nearly the same time I did."

"I run," he said simply. Sergio didn't know diddly what he was doing, but he was doing it better than I was. But not all was well with him.

"Look at my legs," he said. "They're burnt."

I looked at his legs. They were burnt. That's understatement. They'd gone past red to a richer, darker color. If his shanks had been pullet drumsticks on the spit, they'd be past well done.

"Didn't you put on any sunscreen?"

"I should've put on sunscreen."

We'd had day after day of triple-digit sunshine, where solar energy singed like a hot stove. Sergio was seriously burned, and he still had a few days to go. He went out back somewhere, saying something about taking a nap. I finished eating and went back to the road.

I prefer to run alone, to run my own race, to depend on my own strength and not someone else's. And by that comment I don't mean any hostility or criticism of anyone who wants to team up. Running alone is nothing but my own preference.

At times I grew embarrassed at how slowly I was

forced to run. I decided I had to get over that. Who cared whether what I was doing was what anyone would call running? I wouldn't worry with it. I had to get my chafing ass down the road by whatever means my aching feet could muster. It was my race to run, and I'd run it anyway I could. Or not.

Leaving Hampshire two years ago: A black dog I'd not seen or heard launched a stealth attack from behind. I saw him at the last moment. When I spun to face him my momentum tripped me and I slammed the pavement. The violent commotion shocked him and made me angry. He knew he'd messed up. When I jumped up screaming I was going to tear his goddamned head off, he knew it in spades. He lowered his tail and skulked back to the house without a sound.

Jeff Whiteside is a neighborhood man who was driving a new white Ford pickup and wore blue jeans and a short-sleeved plaid cotton shirt. He stopped and handed me a cold bottle of water. He got out of his truck. We talked about how hot it was and we talked about running.

"I've run a half marathon, but nothing like what you're doing."

"You can be a runner without doing anything like this. In fact, I doubt anybody ought to do this."

"It's awful hot. Be careful."

A little while later, he came back along the road again and handed me another frosty bottle of water.

"Thank you so much. It's so hot, a bottle doesn't go very far."

"I know. I'm headed to the cornfield. It's gonna be hot there."

Jeff is a farmer and a runner, worthy endeavors, both. Today he was also a Road Angel.

The route crosses over a four-lane just as runners enter Columbia. Anxious to escape the noise, I trotted across the bridge and kept on running, foot pain notwithstanding. Someone yelled and I looked back. Joe Kowalski was sitting under a shade tree in some rank Bermuda grass against a brush row surrounding a corn field. Sitting in weeds! Joe is a civil engineer from Cincinnati. I sat with him on the bus from Castle Rock to Union City six days earlier. It seemed like a lifetime ago. True engineering nerd, Joe was packing more technology than he needed, including a portable battery charger for his cell phone. That habit also makes him resourceful.

Two years ago, he ran the race when I did. I remember seeing him in the Korner Kafe on the second morning. His feet were in terrible shape already and another unsupported runner was treating his blisters. I felt sorry for his misfortune. Now he was sitting in weeds.

Damn, Joe, there are chiggers there!

But I just waved and kept running. I worked my way along the broken walk and past leaning stone walls that fronted elegant old houses of a bygone era. I had to find the square but the road went straight to it.

There's a sandwich shop in Columbia. It goes by the name Sandwich Shop. It's just off the square. Unimposing, it's just one of the glass storefronts there. Two years ago, unsure of my route, I walked back and forth past it three times before I went in and drank three tall glasses of water with my hamburger before I realized how dehydrated and stupid I'd gotten. This time, I felt like an old customer. The joint is one of the old fashioned kinds of downtown restaurants that serves basic stuff. So, I ordered a burger and fries and sat at the bar watching flies inside bump against the glass and listening to two old gentlemen at a table behind me. The proprietor, a slender old gentleman in glasses, slapped a patty on the griddle and resumed chasing flies with his swatter. He whacked the counter near me and made a sheepish grin.

"Missed him again," he said.

"Yeah, that's easy to do."

One of the men behind me left. The remaining one, a heavy man in bib overalls and maybe three remaining brown front teeth, began talking with me while I ate my burger and fries. He was a good-hearted old gent, but I wasn't in much of a mood for talking.

That was supper. A baloney sandwich and Beanee Weanees in Hampshire for lunch and now burger and fries for supper, actual food, it was my lucky day.

I cut across the courthouse square and headed south. The Vol State route followed an old street next to a wide boulevard. Then it did something else I wasn't sure about and then joined still another old street next to the boulevard. It was hard to tell. I stopped at a shaded spot in a parking lot and studied my city maps—there are two for Columbia: Columbia and Columbia Metro. A drop of water had dissolved the picture on both maps at the place where I was.

So, I had to depend on the tire store. It is called the Best-One Tire Services. It has a big tractor tire standing

outside. When we passed it on the bus, someone had said
that it was important to go either behind the store or in
front of the store. But I couldn't remember which one was
important, front or back. Again, I should have been listening better.

I choose the back, and took a little street that first skirt-
ed the building and then turned and headed south, the
way I wanted to go. But the farther I went the more dismal
it looked, a small old street lined by industrial buildings of
one kind or another. It would take me south and eventually to the hotel I was aiming for, if it didn't dead-end, but I
decided it wasn't the official course and made a U-turn to
get back to where I'd been. The front must have been the
important way. I headed past the front where the big tire
was standing and continued on.

Just a block from the Richland Inn, the hotel where
runners were staying in Columbia, I walked into the Shell
K-W Mart. I needed to get some milk and a granola bar for
breakfast, because I was about to pack it in at the Richland.
If I hadn't spent twenty-five minutes vainly circling the
tire store I would have missed the connection that happened next.

Faulkner may be right. We don't know. The worth-
less rocks are not yet hanging tideless in the last dying
evening, but man's puny voice nonetheless is certainly
talking, and I guess it'll go on like the novelist said. That
last red evening will have to speed up if it hopes to catch
up to the man's voice I was hearing. I knew whose it was,
too. So I rushed to the back of the store and bought a bottle
of water. Then I walked up to the man I hadn't seen in five

days and 150 miles and held out the water to John Sharp.

"Man, I'd like to pay you back for that water you gave me on the first day," I said.

The irrepressible man looked at me and stopped talking for a full ten milliseconds.

"Ahh, we don't want any pay for that. We're glad to help." He was with two other runners, a young woman and a man.

"Well, you may have saved me from the meat wagon. I let myself get into terrible shape and you pulled me out with that water."

"Oh, I'm just glad you're still out here, still going."

He asked me if I was starting out for a night run to the next town. I told him I'd just gotten into Columbia and that I was going up to the hotel for a little sleep.

"Take our room!" he said. "We just left it. We're going back on the road. We checked out but just go ask for John Sharp's room. Tell 'em you're one of the runners. They'll give it to you. It's already paid for."

I came to pay him back for helping me before. But now the man was helping me again, compounding my debt. I thanked them and they went on.

The young woman at the hotel counter was tan and tall and big enough to play basketball. When I asked for John's room, she mumbled some reason why she couldn't give me that particular room, likely because they'd already cleaned it for the next day—I didn't catch the reason. "But I can let you have another room some runners had," she said.

"That'd be fine," I told her.

But it wasn't fine. When I got to the room, I found out that housekeeping had already stripped the beds of all cover and pillow cases. Only bare mattresses remained. Towels were all gone except for one hand towel. At least I could take a shower and wash my clothes.

My raw feet stuck to the tile floor like uncooked pork chops. I didn't look at their bottoms. I knew I couldn't do anything about their condition.

Sleeping was now my problem. I didn't want to lie down nude on the motel mattress, and my clothes were wet. Engineers know how to improvise. It's a trait. But I had little to improvise with. Then a thought hit me. I had a wind jacket. I'd wear it a new way, like a skirt. I wrapped the collar around my waist and zipped the front as high as I could, until it was firm around my waist.

Bedtime. I was at mile 179. I had chafed thighs, a red toe and raw soles. Tomorrow was looking to be interesting.

Chapter Six

Bench of Despair

There are two stories about Columbia that catch your attention when you're running Vol State and you find yourself stepping onto the road in the dark at four o'clock in the morning. The first one is informational and I had put it behind me. My friend Dianne Taylor, who was somewhere behind me and who has finished this event three times, and the one who is maybe responsible for my running it, too—I may re-evaluate our friendship—told me: "Don't go through Columbia at night—drug activity."

I had put it behind me. The motel I was leaving is on the exit side of town, already past the malls and joints and bars. There were scattered businesses ahead, but soon I'd leave them behind and enter the countryside proper.

The second story sounds apocryphal, but I believe it is true because Diane knew the men in the story. They stepped out of the same hotel I had just stayed in and turned the wrong way. After a while they realized they weren't on the right road. But where was the right road?

They called up someone, likely John Price, who knows everything about this race, and he, or somebody, told them which way to go. Only that didn't work either because they weren't actually on the road the advisor thought they were on.

"They spent the whole morning going around and around in Columbia," Diane said.

This raises a scary feature of this race: you must do your own navigation, at least if you are unsupported. Nobody is going to tell you if you make a wrong turn. You might not realize it until you find yourself in the wrong town ten miles off the course. At that point, you also can't hitch a ride back to where you left the course. You must get back under your own power.

That thought served to keep me alert to where I was, and as a practice I tried to identify check points frequently. I was not scared this morning. I'd passed this way before, and I remembered the road. I started down E. James Campbell Boulevard, initially a divided four-lane, also known as State Route 50, confidently but alert. No moonlight helped me now. My stingy friend's favors had fallen out of play, gone hiding behind the horizon. There were some clouds about also. It was darker than past mornings. I pulled out my LED hand-held flashlight, not for navigation so much as to help me avoid road debris or holes that could catastrophically twist an ankle.

First time I passed this way afoot, two years ago, I was a bit more apprehensive. That night was clear and I could see Cassiopeia overhead well enough to know I was going east, which I had to do. I had another check. The course makes a long sweeping turn south. I saw that turn coming via approaching car lights before I got to it.

Odd what you remember. As the road made its turn a side street intersected. It doesn't hurt to double-check. I put my light on the street sign: Mapleash Avenue. That strange name struck me. I read it like "Map Leash." It sounded like some goofy internet name or password, a strange new word made from the combination of two other words. When I tried to look it up, I found out that it most likely comes from a tree named Maple Ash, a local tree sometimes called a box elder (which if you combine would become boxelder).

Could it have been then a box elder, or maple ash, that originated the most distinct memory I'd taken away from that run two years earlier, a sound I'd not heard in sixteen years that stopped me in my tracks, head cocked? The sound of two years ago came again, music that yanked me back to the farm sixty years past: a whip-poor-will. On the farm those birds called from a hackberry tree on the hill, a tree that was convenient. Maybe here the maple ash is most convenient. In any case the bird sat calling just a few minutes after the Mapleash sign. I would never know the bird's perch tree, only its call. It buoyed me that morning.

My light was dimming from battery drain when I reached the Mapleash sign this time, but I had to confirm the sign just for memory's sake. I trotted on down the road listening for the expected bird call, but it was all quiet this morning. That was a loss, but I had heard whip-poor-wills on three other mornings of this run, at places where I didn't hear them two years ago. That was my consolation.

Shortly after recalling this sweet memory there occurred the most shocking, humiliating and dispiriting event of the whole run: I shit my pants.

It was the pair of shorts out of which I'd cut the bottom of the liner. How on earth?

As I trotted south, the sky began to grow light. I thought I'd better look for a place to poop while I still had dusk for cover. I came to where a driveway of coarse crusher gravel went through the bush row. It looked like some kind of seldom-used access road to a farm or utility, and it was chained off with a no trespassing sign hanging on the chain. In that opening through the bushes, I had cover, especially since it was still nearly dark and there was almost no traffic on Route 50. At the edge of the gravel the surface sloped and I couldn't squat completely without losing balance. I pulled my shorts only part way down and deposited runny droppings—at least I'd been drinking enough water.

I had a napkin from the Sandwich Shop I'd removed from my pack. I nearly always carry a napkin or two. I tore it into four rectangles and wiped, throwing the pieces on the ground. Then I pulled my pants up. I wasn't going to leave the paper litter. I cut a bough from a pine tree and sharpened the end. My handy penknife saves the day. Then I speared each of the soiled pieces of paper onto the stick like a shish kabob. I parted the dense boughs of the pine tree and shoved the paper shish kabob deep down into the tree foliage. No one will ever see those pieces of paper. I was proud of my tidy cleanup.

As I walked across the road, I began to notice a sour

smell. And I felt something wet running down my leg. Somehow I had missed the ground and shit in my shorts. At least part of the runny stuff had missed the ground and ended up in my shorts. Which I'd pulled back up in complete innocence. Exactly how that unprecedented event happened I've not figured out. I guess I never will. Despite my neat cleanup, I now walked down the road with a dollop of runny shit in my pants. It was beginning to run down my leg.

Everyone poops. But not in their pants. This was a first. Naturally, I was aghast and distraught—and wondering what I was going to do to get cleaned up.

That's when the sheriff passed me and pulled his SUV over on the shoulder. He sat waiting in his Chevy for me to approach. The window came down.

"How you doing? Are you okay?" And so on, that was his bit.

"Fine," I lied through my teeth. I stood there talking to him like a normal person would, but feeling like shit and smelling like shit. Maybe he smelled it too, because suddenly he needed to get on down the road.

But I held him a little longer. It was all very professional.

"I've been looking for highway 373. Is it coming up soon?"

"It's just ahead. If you watch my tail lights, you'll see me turn."

"I thought it ought to be. It seemed like I'd come far enough, but I hadn't seen a sign. I've been watching."

"It's just ahead. You'll see me turn."

"Thank you. I appreciate it."

And, son, if you can stand straight up and talk to The Man while a load of fresh shit reeks in your britches and runs down your leg, what in this world could ever scare you?

See, what I was counting on was the Bench of Despair. It resides at Glendale Market, which comes a mile after the course turns off 50 onto 373. "Despair" was the right word. "Desperation" was, too. If the Bench of Despair couldn't save me, it was going to be creek water. And I didn't even know where a creek was.

I remembered well visiting Glendale Market on my last run. It was early in the morning that time, too. I bought two sausage-biscuits and filled up my water bottles. Afterwards, I went striding down the road eating that last sandwich and singing Beethoven's "Bench of Joy."

Bench of Despair. It has some kind of mythic significance. I think it is that if a runner manages to make it past that inviting sit-down place, he will most likely finish the race. It suggests that you don't sit down on it and get seduced by the restful bliss of reposing thereon. I didn't sit on it at all two years ago. I stood over it holding thumb down, in an attitude of scorn, while someone made a picture.

Bench of Despair. It's made of wood and looks like a church pew someone stole. It sits outside the front of the market, glowing deep blood red. Black stenciled letters on the backrest say what it is: Bench of Despair. Beware the Bench of Despair, I say.

It was a happier time, that last time I ran past the

Bench of Despair. I was singing the happy blues. But this time, this time, my friend, I was singing the shitty blues.

This time I angled past the Bench of Despair trailing an invisible plume of foul fragrance. I marched into the store and up to the counter. I asked one of the ladies if the restroom was open, and she said it was. It was on the end outside around the corner.

Inside it, I stripped down and stood naked washing my clothes and myself. I'd sat momentarily on the commode seat. I had to wash it, too. I used paper towels for wash rags, and I used lots of them. I felt like I'd never feel clean again. So, I washed and double washed. I washed my ass off. Finally, I decided I'd done the best I could with what I had and put the wet clothes back on.

Now I smelled okay. I went inside the store. It seems to be run by four ladies and no men that you'd notice. I bought a sausage and biscuit, two bottles of Gatorade and a four-pack of triple-A batteries for my flashlight. I paid and then laid a five dollar tip on the counter. I wondered if they knew why. I put in two new batteries and stowed the two extras in my pack.

This time I did sit on the Bench of Despair. It can't corrupt me. One of the helpers, a young woman about twenty-something came out and sat with me, talking while she took a smoke. I was always glad for company. One of the other ladies came out and asked if I wanted her to make a picture of me, so I handed her my phone.

These ladies try to help runners. They'd placed bottles of water outside for runners that passed in the night before they open. They love the Vol State runners and make them welcome. We buy stuff and love them back.

The two ladies went back inside. I sat resting just a bit more. Suddenly, an impulse hit me. I pointed the phone camera at my face and stuck my tongue out as far as I could à la KISS and made a picture. It was a silly thing to do. The shocking gesture expressed disdain for the red bench the old man was sitting on. If it was a symbol of failure, I wasn't going to honor it. The picture showed no trace of the humility you'd expect from a man who'd just washed poop out of his britches. I uploaded the rude image to Twitter and posted it on Facebook later that day with the caption, "Gene Simmons retires, grows white beard, runs #VolState500K, mocks Bench of Despair."

Joshua Holmes, founder of Run It Fast, was following the race each day. He called the photo the best one produced by Vol State. It was the ugliest one. Maybe it was the most unusual. But it expressed how I felt at the time.

I rested too long. A young man drove up in a truck. He'd mounted a flag pole on the truck bed that held a three-foot Confederate flag. The flag drooped and hung limp once he stopped. He talked briefly with an older customer at the gas pump and then went inside. Wonder how many Confederate Generals the ill-mannered man could name?

The bottom of my feet hurt as I headed on down the road. I knew blisters were developing and growing. The split I'd cut in my shoe had solved the toe problem, however. It no longer pressed my toe at all. But a new irritation developed. The right shoe was hurting my outside ankle bone.

It was easy to figure out why. We traveled on the left side of the road, which slopes toward the ditch. That causes the shoe to lean slightly in that direction, so that the top lip presses a bit harder just below the ankle bone. It should not have been happening. It didn't happen on my last run, where I was using the same brand and model. To solve the problem, I loosened the top laces and spread the top of the shoes open a bit more.

That solved the ankle problem, but may have allowed more foot movement in the shoe and aggravated the blisters forming on my soles. I didn't think of that at the time. I'd solved two foot problems. That left only one and it was a big one: blistering on the bottom. All I could do for that was take the advice I'd given Jameelah back in Linden: Put Body Glide on it and go on.

Before I reached Culleoka—a name I love, Indian word, I guess—I encountered Road Angels. A sign made of hand-lettered white poster board on the roadside announced, "Road Angel ahead." Sure enough, a young woman had erected a tent for shade and placed fruit and cold drinks in a cooler.

I stopped in. Her name was Kim Nutt and she was aided by her young son Graham, a handsome little boy with a soccer ball. We stood in their front yard.

"Do you play soccer?" I asked him.

A nod.

"Yeah? Let me see you kick it. Drop it and kick it." He dropped the ball and kicked the fool out of it.

"Yeah! That boy can kick. I'll say, he can!"

Kim's sense of service toward runners amazed me.

She had gone to a lot of trouble. She was a sweet person, to boot. I asked how it happened that she wanted to be a Road Angel. She described a previous year, when it was raining. She'd been to town and upon returning saw an older woman walking in the rain near her house.

"She looked so miserable! I invited her into the house. All I had to give her was some left-over pizza. But you would have thought I gave her the best thing in the world. She appreciated it so much. It just touched me, and after that I wanted to help more runners."

I asked her if we could make a selfie. She hoisted Graham and I aimed my camera, photographing the three of us. The resulting picture, Kim, Graham and me, all smiling is as sweet as my last picture was sour. Kim and Graham helped me. I know they helped lots of runners. Kim added me as a friend on Facebook later that day. I saw one of her comments. She said she was sure I'd touch The Rock! With that encouragement, I had to try hard.

You come to the Mooresville Market a couple of miles before you pass under I-65. I remembered that and was looking forward to seeing that store. It is one of the old-fashioned framed box stores with squeaky oiled wood floors. I marched in and asked the lady if she had a chocolate-covered vanilla Popsicle. I wanted a Brown Mule. We went to a cooler in the back and she produced that very item. I sat on the front porch eating the ice cream. It was hot outside and the Popsicle was melting fast enough a few drops fell off before I could wolf it all down.

In Lewisburg sleep began to catch up with me. I stopped at a market and had some fried chicken for lunch.

I ate it sitting outside. A mile later I sat on a curb downtown. I dreaded going on. My feet hurt badly, but I dragged on. At what seemed the last chance before leaving Lewisburg, I went into a Shell market for a bottle of water. I wanted to start on the long country stretch ahead with full bottles. When I came out, two young women were standing on the walk, one a runner, one a crew. The crew member was smearing sunscreen on the runner.

Ally Gregory was the runner. I remembered seeing her before the race started, but had not seen her since. Her arms and legs are decorated with tattoos. She was wearing a trucker hat and a ring in her septum. We walked along together for a while. Talking with her took my mind off my burning soles. She told me her name.

"It's Ally, like the space between two buildings."

Her crew was Mindy, her wife, she told me. Actually, I'd spoken with Mindy just as I was entering Lewisburg, where she'd parked to wait for her runner.

Just weeks earlier the Supreme Court had struck down bans on same-sex marriage. I wanted to ask Ally if she and Mindy had gotten married in Tennessee—she lives in Knoxville—since that Supreme Court decision, or if they'd gotten married earlier in a state that permitted it. I wanted to ask, but I didn't want to intrude. Instead, we went along talking about running problems, how one had to be flexible and able to change in response to arising problems. I told her how I'd changed my shoe lacing to solve my ankle pain.

It went like that. I liked her and wished our visit could've lasted longer. But soon we reached where Mindy had parked and Ally's younger brother came jogging down the walk to see what she needed. We said bye and I went on alone.

Alone again, I marched up a two-lane that offered only narrow escape lanes. Oncoming traffic was heavy. Further from town, it would thin, I figured.

This stretch of road holds one of the most endearing memories of my first Vol State run. I needed water that day two years ago. I saw a man under dense oak shade trees in the yard of a house. I headed across his lawn. As I got closer, I saw that he was an aged black man, leaning on a cane. I saw a garden hose coiled at the house foundation. I held up an empty bottle.

"Do you mind if I get some water at the faucet?"

"I've got some cold water."

"Well, the faucet would be fine."

"I'll get you some cold water. On the carport."

He was determined, I saw. He walked unsteadily toward me. When he reached the walk, there was a five inch step-up. He hesitated and planted his cane. I watched, afraid he'd fall. He shifted his weight to the cane and in a flicker set his foot up on the walk, barely clearing it. I followed him into the carport. There was a door to a utility room.

"I built this house," he said.

"It's a good house. You did a good job."

He opened the utility room door. "See my tools?" He'd mounted a plywood panel on the back of the door. It was filled with hooks where his tools hung. I admired his tools.

He opened a refrigerator in the little room and handed me two bottles of icy water. He motioned toward the carport floor as we stepped out of the room.

"See the cart I made to carry them in?"

It was a wooden shipping crate like those once used for fragile equipment or heavy machine components. He'd mounted wheels on the crate so that he could roll it to where he needed to work.

I could have stayed and talked a long time—only I couldn't. I still think about the old man now and then. I think he told me he was eighty-seven. I could tell he'd worked hard. I wish I could see him again and tell him that he helped me. He was more than a Road Angel. In sharing his water, he shared his life.

This run, I missed the old gentleman's house. I couldn't remember exactly where it was, traffic distracted me, my burning soles distracted me and storm clouds began to gather. We were about to get a break in the unrelenting heat that had cooked Sergio's legs, burned the back of my neck, that had pooled the sweat in my shoes and aided the blister-causing slipping. We were due a break.

State Route 64 peeled off to the right of Route 31 and headed toward Shelbyville, twenty-six miles away. Sleepiness was overtaking me. I had to find a place for a nap. The Farmington Church of Christ appeared a mile after the intersection. There was a covered picnic area, with tables and a concrete floor. Lord, that's all I need, a smooth concrete floor.

I jerked my pack off, made it into a pillow, stretched out on the cool smoothness and pulled my running hat over my face. It was that easy. I was asleep, unaware of the minutes racing by, of the building storm clouds. I was unconscious.

The world exploded in my face, with blinding light and the howling roar of sudden wind. My hat was in the grass. The squall had hit suddenly. I dashed out for my hat. A downpour started and then grew. Wind swept spray through the open shelter. My nap was over. I started getting cold. I put on my windbreaker.

What luck! I had already been under shelter when the storm I didn't even know was coming had hit. I stood as far toward the shelter's leeward side as possible and waited out the rain. As it tapered off a bit a maroon van pulled boldly across the grassy yard and parked beside my pad. It was Jan in Meat Wagon. I believe she would find me if I was on the moon. But, no thanks. I don't need the meat wagon. My burning feet do, but I don't. Jan sat and talked a bit and then drove on.

Eventually, the rain backed off altogether and I headed down the road again. Soon the windbreaker came off. It wasn't as hot as before but the moisture was like steam.

I swear people will help you. Coming up was a frame house on the left, a young woman in the yard with her three kids, two girls and a boy who was the youngest. The oldest girl, maybe seven had a pitcher of water. Their mother was giving them a lesson in charity and sharing. I bet they remember it. I held down a bottle and let the little girl pour it full and then thanked her profusely. I should have given the kids a dollar apiece, but didn't think of it. Soon the father rode up on a kids' bike, one with little wheels. He looked to be of Middle-Eastern descent. I would have been fine without the water, but the incident in Dogwood Park has never left me. If someone wants to help me, I can't deny them that simple human pleasure, especially a kid.

Soon it would be dark. I realized I needed something to eat. It was going to be late by the time I reached Shelbyville. I came to a country market I didn't know existed, the Pit Stop. Inside the store, only a few sandwiches were left in the glass cabinet, all wrapped in aluminum foil. I pointed to one.

"I think that hamburger with a bunch of mustard on it would be good." The lady unwrapped the sandwich and squirted mustard on like I'd said, wrapped it back up and handed it to me. I reached out a ten dollar bill. She shook her head.

"I don't want any money for it. I want to give it to you."

"But I can pay. You can't make a living giving…"

"I don't need any money for it. You keep it," she said.

Here was a woman who makes her living selling food and she wouldn't take any money for the burger. She exemplified the kindness and charity I'd encountered all along. It was enough to spoil a cynic, corrupt him and convert him to an optimistic Pollyanna.

The lesson was plain: I'd traveled back roads, freeways and city streets alike, alone and at night for much of the time, roads people are afraid to even drive without a loaded gun in the console. What I found was kindness. Simple human kindness. That lesson needs shouting.

It began to grow dark. I could see silhouettes of storm clouds against the fading sky light. Jagged streaks of lightning stabbed and slashed the dark. I stopped and posted a tweet: "Lightning streaks flashing all around and I'm the highest thing sticking up on this highway." I walked on, studying the heavens: not time to seek shelter yet. Then my phone pinged. An ultrarunner in England had clicked the "like" button on my post. The unexpected response flushed me with a warm feeling not unlike love. A man a quarter of the way around the world was at that minute sharing, in some small way, my experience. His spirit accompanied me.

I'd had a more intense experience with social media two years earlier, at the 2013 Boston Marathon, the year of the bombing. I crossed the finish line a few minutes before the blast. A young Pakistani woman I follow was monitoring the marathon that day. She immediately sent me a private message asking if I was okay. A journalist, she covers human-rights stories for *Dawn*, Pakistan's largest newspaper. Bombings and massacres are the stuff of her professional life. Yet, from half way around the globe her digital voice reached me, asking about my safety. In that moment I felt like she was a precious friend.

Social media have pushed back the sight horizons for me, expanding my view of the world and my place in it.

My trudge dragged on. Would Shelbyville ever appear? My whole being was consumed by two things—my burning soles and a nagging need to sleep. I came to a crude driveway sloping down to a soybean field. It was made of wasted concrete, poured out to get rid of it, and only partially smoothed. I stretched out on it. But it was no good. The surface was too lumpy and cars made too much noise. A decent place to sleep could only be found if I kept going toward Shelbyville. I got up and marched on.

I knew where a hotel was in Shelbyville. I stopped in a market shortly before the hotel to get some food for supper and breakfast. It wasn't midnight but it was late. The market was empty. The clerk, a long-haired young man, was outside having a smoke. He followed me in, curious about my running get-up at such a time of day. He asked the usual questions and expressed the usual amazement when I told him what I was up to. I told him that if I could finish I'd be the oldest ever.

"I bet you'll make it." He didn't know I stood there in the soup of oozing raw feet.

I headed on up the street toting a plastic bag of Beanee Weenees, banana, milk and so on until I came to a broad intersection where I had to leave the course to go a couple blocks to the hotel. This is the place where I'd lost all my maps two years earlier. I didn't realize I'd lost them until I reached the hotel that night.

That was a huge problem. Of course I had the maps stored in my phone. I'd have to use those digital maps, but that drains the battery quickly, plus the screen is hard to read in bright daylight. I'd just have to make do. Next morning I left the hotel to come back to the course. When I got to the intersection, there laid my maps in their plastic bags. They had lain there all night just where I left them. That was lucky.

The fact that they were in that place also answered

the question about how I'd lost them in the first place. Phil Min, crewing for Diane Bolton, of the "poor dallas" check-in call, was at the intersection when I'd come through. I was carrying a bag of food that night, too. I set it down and chatted with him while I waited for the light to change. I set the bag down on my maps, apparently. When the light changed I grabbed the bag, but forgot the maps. That was two years earlier. I'd not make that mistake again.

This time at the hotel I still had possession of my maps. By the time I took a shower and ate some supper, it was nearly midnight. I'd come forty-four miles—on feet growing more and more like raw meat, putrid raw meat. I didn't bother looking; I could tell by how they hurt and stuck to the tile.

Oddly, the toe no longer bothered me. Splitting the shoe had done the trick. I knew I'd lose the toenail. If I'd only made the correction earlier, I would have saved the nail.

It was colorful, the toe. A white band of pus just under the skin bordered the root. The purple nail was surrounded by inflamed red flesh. Purple and red make a killer color match. Most people don't know that. I once had some red warmup pants I'd wear with a purple shirt. It was one of my favorite combos. But you don't see people matching purple and red very much. My toe didn't know that.

It was too late and I was too tired to write a blog story. I went for a shorter message. I liked the toe so much I made a close up and uploaded it to Facebook with the simple caption, "I trusted those shoes."

Photos

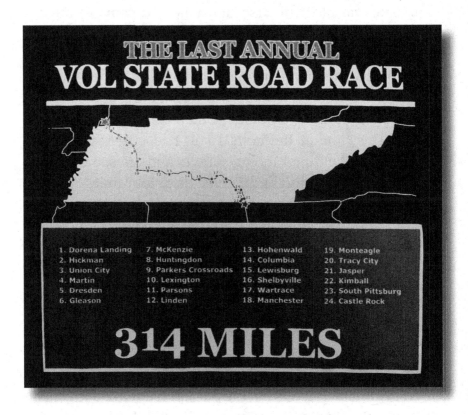

The design on my 2015 VOL STATE tee-shirt
illustrates the race course.

Members of the Run It Fast club pose for a photo while waiting for the race to start. Greg Armstrong (without shirt) from Lebanon, Tennessee, a supported runner, became King of the Road for a second consecutive year, winning in a time of 3d 22h 05m 20s.

*I stand in Hickman, Kentucky at the edge of floodwater
from the Mississippi River, July 9, 2015.*

The author and Lazarus Lake ride the Dorena Landing-Hickman Ferry two years earlier, July 11, 2013.

The Middle Fork of the Obion River north of Gleason, Tennessee suggests a jungle-like wilderness.

Sergio Bianchini and Lynda Webber enjoy breakfast at the Korner Kafe in Gleason, Tennessee on the second morning of our run.

Uber-marathon couple Cathie and Troy
Johnson rest in Clarksburg, Tennessee.

The sun rises over the Tennessee River
in West Tennessee on the third
morning of the run.

Johan Steene from Stockholm, Sweden, slouches on the Bench of Despair
during our bus stop at Glendale Market for lunch on the day before the race start. His relaxed demeanor belies his extraordinary durance capability. He finished in 3d 23h 15m 50s, the first unsupported runner, barely more than an hour behind overall winner Greg Armstrong.

Mocking the Bench of Despair even while I sit on it expresses the disdain I feel.

The town square of Wartrace, Tennessee provides a safe place for little kids to ride their bikes— also where I took a mid-morning nap.

The skeleton of a once stately elm, likely killed by Dutch Elm Disease, stands beside a two-lane route of the most unusual name—16th Model Road.

*Both times I ran Vol State, Lana Sain
came out to meet me in her hometown of
Manchester, Tennessee.*

Some 190 miles after crossing it in West Tennessee,
we cross the Tennessee River again, in East Tennessee,
on a span referred to after its paint job as:
The "Blue Bridge."

*A dusty farm road stretches through a corn field
near the finish line at Castle Rock, Georgia.*

L to R, the author, Diane Bolton, Joshua Holmes, and David Wingard pose at the ledge called The Rock, visible at left, on my first Vol State finish, July 19, 2013 (photo courtesy of Joshua Holmes).

Jameelah Abdul-Rahim Mujaahi and I shared some anxious moments when we both ran out of water on the first day. By happenstance, the day after finishing, we meet again, in Kimball, Tennessee.

Chapter Seven

Road Angels

I had a small day ahead. After forty-four miles the previous day, I was looking to pick up just twenty-nine today, on a trek to Manchester. I stepped out on the street later than normal. It was full daylight before I trudged out of Shelbyville. First town would be Wartrace.

My feet were shredded, the thick tough skin now delaminated from the main sole like a flap with tattered edges. Each toe was injured in a similar way, just over a smaller area. I walked in a stew of ooze. I knew this even without a lingering inspection. The damage was done now. Like Jameelah's blistered feet in Linden on day four, or Sergio's burnt legs on day five in Hampshire, it was too late to prevent it. Now I just had to figure out how to live with it. I could've wrapped my feet with duct tape, like the guy did his scrotum. I've seen feet so wrapped in ultra-marathons. But I didn't have duct tape. Might have been able to find it at markets, but I didn't seriously consider that strategy.

My solution was simple, same as I'd told Jameelah: Put Body Glide on it and go on. That's what I did. There was a problem with even that: My stick of Body Glide was running out so that I had to use it sparingly. I'd bought a women-sized stick before I started the trip, aiming to reduce my pack to a minimum. Now it was nearly gone. I'd cut it too close.

The solution to chafed thighs had worked like a charm. Cutting the bottom out of the brief worked. Only I knew that a nickel's worth of flimsy fabric hung between me and indecency. It was enough. Now that I understand the chafing mechanism better, I realize I might have saved my shorts from mutilation by applying Body Glide directly to the brief, and in greater amounts. But then again, my Body Glide had been running low.

Surprises aren't surprising any more. A few miles short of Wartrace a man stood on the shoulder ahead watching my approach. He was wearing a small yellow helmet that looked like a kid's model. The chin straps hung down. He told me he was a federal agent.

"I can go anywhere and inspect. I'm the only one can do that."

"Huh...," I affirmed with a nod.

"You need anything, you just call me."

"I'm hoping I can make it to Manchester this evening."

"I can go anywhere. You don't have to worry about that. I'm a federal agent."

A motor scooter sat nearby, which I supposed was the reason for the helmet.

"You can call me. I have authority to go anywhere. I can go in that house right there." He motioned toward a derelict frame house behind him that looked like it had been long-time deserted.

"Uh-huh."

"See, I'm a federal agent. See right here." He held a driver's license out and pointed at a code on it. "See right there?" I glanced at it, but I didn't take the time to read the details. It looked like a driver's license.

"I can go anywhere with that. I'm authorized. You call me if you need any help."

He never mentioned his phone number. But I wasn't going to call anybody anyway, unless it was a question of life or death. I started edging away, up the shoulder, with him still telling me he was a federal agent, and that I should call him if I needed anything.

I didn't go many miles until another man stood waiting beside his pickup. He knew me. We had talked once, maybe twice, at the RC Cola and Moon Pie ten-mile race in the quaint little town of Bell Buckle, which is nearby. But he had to tell me his name, Jason Reeves.

"I live in Bell Buckle," he told me. "I work at Farm Bureau in Shelbyville and this morning I took a different route to work hoping I'd catch you."

"What an honor! You went out of your way. I appreciate that."

Jason is a runner too, and he'd noticed my running in local races. I told Jason about the strange man who claimed to be a federal agent. Jason didn't know him. The strange man seemed like someone everybody nearby would know. Later I asked Laz, who lives near Wartrace, if he knew who the man was. He didn't know him either.

I thanked Jason for coming out to meet me. "Thanks so much! You've got a good career and a good place to live, too," I told him. The day was getting on. I had to get on too.

A Marathon Station—good name for it!—sat on the right as I entered Wartrace. I went in and re-filled my bottles and, since my Body Glide was nearly gone, looked for Vaseline. It was on a display next to the condoms. Figures. Then I went looking for something to eat.

"I guess I'll have a sausage and biscuit, something I can eat on the go," I told the lady clerk.

"Why? Do you have to eat it on your own time?" I thought about that a second, and I didn't know anybody else's time I could use and so I figured I'd have to use my own. I didn't say that but instead answered,"The clock never stops." It's a tough master, the clock. The road goes on forever and the clock never stops. I left with the sandwich.

In the last few miles the road into Wartrace is joined by the Strolling Jim race course. It's familiar. I've run Strolling Jim twice. The finish line to the forty-mile race is in front of the Walking Horse Hotel, behind which Strolling Jim, the first world-champion walking horse, is buried. The hotel is the cue to turn right onto Church Street, which turns into Knob Creek Road. Miss this turn, and you'll end up badly off course.

A gazebo sits on the town square. It's a peaceful place. A little boy and girl were riding their bikes around on the square. It's the kind of place where kids can do that. It was too peaceful. I stretched out in the gazebo and took a twelve-minute nap.

Leaving Wartrace, a roadside display featuring a rail fence and a log cabin is the cue to turn left onto a small two-lane called Knob Creek Road—which, actually is the name of the road you're already on. Anyway, do not miss this turn, Vol State runner. It's easy to do. The main road goes on and you don't expect to turn onto such a small road. I even saw an arrow on the main road indicating straight on ahead. That arrow is in fact for the Strolling Jim race, which does continue on ahead. I know a guy that followed that arrow two years ago.

You want Knob Creek. It was my favorite road of the whole blooming 314-mile course. It goes up a narrowing valley and Knob Creek burbles beside the road, part of which is shaded. Race director Lazarus Lake, aka Gary Cantrell, lives a couple miles up this road.

The road holds a bittersweet memory from my first Vol State run. I passed the house of Amanda Floyd. Her dear friend Diane Taylor—she was somewhere behind me—had told me which house it is. It's a neat traditional white farmhouse, reminiscent of an earlier era. I noted it and trudged on. A little further up the road, and a neighborhood gentleman stopped his pickup to talk with me.

"Gary Cantrell is gonna kill you runners, ain't he?" That was a conversation opener.

"I may be dying right now." We laughed and talked. His name was Gary Floyd he told me. And his wife was a runner, he said. Her name was Amanda.

"I know Amanda!" I exclaimed. "I just passed her house—your house. And I know her friend Diane Taylor."

This was a fascinating connection for me. It happens that I'd met Amanda at her very first race, in 2004, the Race Judicata 5k that ran up the face of a mountain in West Nashville. Diane Taylor had brought her to that race, and I chided her for bringing Amanda to such a hard race for her very first attempt. After that Amanda quickly increased her distances, and I'd see her regularly at area races. In fact, only a month earlier she'd run the RC Cola and Moon Pie ten-mile race, where I'd talked with her.

Gary Floyd, whom I'd never met before, sat in his truck and I stood in the road relating those stories of his wife to him. No traffic disturbed us.

Now, as my burning feet carried me in a faltering stride up the same road, I was remembering those events from two years earlier, the talk with Gary. It is etched forever in my memory. Because the sad part is Amanda died suddenly just three months after I'd met her husband here. She died while running due to a heart defect she didn't know about. It may have been on this very road, since she lived on it. I don't know. She was fifty-three.

On the run this time, a little past where I'd talked with Gary two years earlier, a car stopped and a slender middle-aged man with a ponytail got out. A young woman passenger stepped out the other side. The man said he knew race director Gary Cantrell.

"So ya'll are out enjoying a father-daughter adventure today."

"No." Whoops. I'd guessed wrong. She looked pretty

young, but she wasn't his daughter.

"Oh, sorry."

The young woman just smiled. I was climbing the hill at the end of the valley. They told me that a Road Angel had set up a tent with drinks and food somewhere up on top.

"You can't miss it," he said.

It worries me when someone says that. It normally means I'll miss it. If I *could* find it, it was good news. I remembered that stretch from last time and how it was hard to find water. A homeowner had filled one of my bottles from a garden hose. It tasted like rubber. I couldn't drink it. I thanked the couple and trudged on.

Once I left Bedford County and entered Coffee County, Knob Creek Road changed its name to one of the strangest names on the course, "16th Model Road"—which I have to rank ahead of Mapleash in Columbia. The road rolled on over whatever plateau I now traveled. I found the Road Angel's tent. It truly was hard to miss, setting in the edge of a neatly mowed hay field. No one was around. I had no one to thank, but I was grateful. I filled my bottles and ate some crackers and watched a man on a tractor raking hay in a nearby field. I wondered if he'd set out the tent, coolers and food.

My map showed I'd soon intersect U.S. 41, which I'd follow into Manchester and beyond. I was anxious. I'd solved the chafing problem, but I still had two strikes against me—a sleeping sickness I couldn't shake and the burning soles on my feet which kept me from making any speed. I couldn't afford a third strike. The meat wagon knew. It circled back to me like a buzzard. Jan stopped in the road and we talked a bit. But I wasn't yet ready to surrender. I hadn't seen her the previous day, although I'd guess she saw me.

I found a church on U.S. 41 that had a picnic area with a concrete floor. I stretched out on it and took a nap. You do what you can. Maybe it would help with one of my problems. Soon I was going again.

As I approached Manchester U.S. 41 became a divided four-lane. I ran facing traffic. I came to a bridge under renovation, and there happened one of the most touching Road Angel incidents of my run. It made me happy and sad both, happy for the noble spirit of humanity, sad for its plight.

The bridge ordinarily carried two lanes of traffic. But one lane was closed and all the traffic was constricted to one lane. Concrete barriers set end to end lined the open lane on one side, the existing handrail on the other. It was like a concrete channel, maybe twelve feet wide, through which the traffic flowed. The going-home traffic was pouring out of town, coming straight at me.

I was reluctant to head into that channel against the flow. It was narrow and there was no escape in case of a distracted driver. I didn't see a feasible alternative. A long detour was out of the question. I waited for a traffic gap and went in, hugging the concrete wall on my left. Soon traffic started again. I stopped running and pressed up against the concrete wall until the next gap. Then I ran forward again. It took a few repeats of that procedure. Most drivers saw my plight and gave as much room as they could.

During one of my dashes, I vaguely noticed a figure

sprint across the traffic and jump the wall at the far end of the bridge. That area was like home plate. I'd be declared safe there—if I made it. The channel widened out and vanished a ways beyond.

The bridge wasn't very long. After a few tries I made it. Then I saw the figure I'd noticed before. He was a young Mexican man in a white shirt and straw hat, one of the construction workers. He was standing on the other side of the barrier, brown face spread in a wide smile, reaching an icy bottle of water out to me. Rushing across traffic, jumping the barrier to get water for the strange runner had seemed a great pleasure to him.

I thanked him, took the bottle of water and went on. I don't even know if he spoke English. I'll always remember his smiling face, his kindness. He likely works for minimum wage. He was there in the hot sun because he had to be to make a living. I was there for my own selfish reasons. Yet, he was the one showing charity, showing kindness. Isn't that always the case? Those who have the least share the most.

Next stop would be the courthouse. Chances are Vol State won't kill you, although it surely could. But it gets in your head and stays there like a noisy upstairs neighbor. It fills your mind with stories that bang around. You sink into a vague abstraction.

I am sitting on a parapet wall in the shade in front of the empty courthouse near the end of the day. The sun is still hot, like standing too close to the stove. The shade is cool, the parapet the right height. It was too tempting. So I sat down to rest. I sit recalling.

My run turned bad the previous day, when I soiled my pants three miles from The Bench of Despair. I was able to clean up and wash off at Glendale Market, but the incident was humiliating and demoralizing, enfeebling in a way. It marks the beginning of my decline. My sleepiness, low energy and foot pain have gone south since then. Now, a day later, I sit on the parapet, demoralized and making zero forward progress.

An older model Ranger pulls into one of the empty parking spaces near where I rest and a man gets out. He's a runner who I recognize, but he tells me his name anyway and we shake hands. His name is Mark Yother. I see his brother Tracy often at local races around my Cookeville home.

"Is there anything I can do?"

"No, sir, just sit here and talk to me while I rest a minute. That's all I need."

I've been alone so much it is good to talk with someone. Mark came to my town and ran a half marathon that I sponsored two years ago. He was running with Lana Sain that day, another Manchester runner. We three ran together a bit. Then they split off for the half and I continued on the marathon course that day.

He is the chief of police here, he tells me. I didn't know that. He was in court all day today. After court, he went home and changed out of his suit and into slacks and shirt and came back into town on the chance of seeing me pass through. From following the race online he knew roughly where I was.

We talk, sitting on the parapet. Because it presses on my mind, I tell him how, on the very first day, some good ole boys in a country transmission shop in West Tennessee saved my run and the run of another runner with me at the time, Jameelah, a young black woman raised in Brooklyn. We'd both run out of water, gotten dehydrated and were suffering leg cramps, losing ability to even hunt water when we walked into their shop. I tell Mark the whole story.

They gave us cold water and cold Gatorade, freely and gladly. The drinks let us recover enough to go on. They saved us from the meat wagon, I tell him.

I'm grateful enough I want to tell everyone, the chief included, about those folks. And proud, too. In the midst of controversy about the Confederate Flag and increasing news of black men being unjustly shot by white policemen, the good ole boys in Tennessee helped the black woman as freely as they helped me. That distinct fact impresses me. I'm proud. And I want to emphasize the equality and generosity of their behavior.

"They helped the Brooklyn-raised black woman just as quickly as they helped the old white Tennessean!" I exclaim to the chief.

"That's the way it ought to be," Mark answers quietly.

I sit resting on the parapet with a police chief like every town ought to have.

I needed to get on through town, to where I-24 passes through before I could rest properly, in a hotel. I said goodbye to Chief Mark and continued my trudge. Soon I was passing car lots and restaurants, getting close. I walked up on a surprise. Here loitered Don Winkley and Crew, standing casually beside their white van. They passed me days ago, just after Linden. I figured they'd gone on way ahead and that I'd never see them again.

"How you doing?" they wanted to know.

I went into a whiny story about how my toe was inflamed and about how the soles of my feet hurt, involuntarily wincing as I shifted weight. Oddly, the sole hurt worse when I lifted my foot. I suppose it was because the motion applied interlaminar tensile stress, tending to further pull the delaminated slab away from the substrate.

"We had a girl—now I tell you this," Don began apologetically, and I assumed he was talking about someone he knows in their running group back home. "Her feet got like yours and she kept going. It got infected and she lost her foot."

That was a scary story for someone who'd been walking in serum for a couple of days. Don assumed a sense of authority and continued.

"What you better do is get some hydrogen peroxide and disinfect them—my feet. Mix it about twenty percent with water and soak them in it."

"Mix it. Where? You mean in the bathtub?"

"Well, yeah, that'd work, but motel trash can is better. Take the plastic liner out. How big's your foot?"

I wanted to resist this advice. I'd be finished soon. I just had a little over sixty miles to go, and I didn't have a van to run all over town looking for a drug store. Don and

Crew sensed my skepticism and told me I could find peroxide in markets. Crew knew someone who worked with a brain surgeon.

"They even wash the brain in peroxide, it's so mild, it won't hurt you," he said.

It was good advice. Don is a veteran ultrarunner. He knew what he was talking about. But I'm just used to enduring stuff and I didn't want any more complications. After we parted, their advice continued to nag me. Why is there always some damned thing to aggravate?

I trudged along what you'd call the main drag, approaching I-24. This is a town of surprises. Next to the folks in West Tennessee—Tom Silver, Marie Threadgill and her daughter Ella Wish—ambushing me with surprise visits, the greatest surprise of my run two years ago had happened in this town.

I'd been limping into town with a foot I'd injured by stepping on a stone a day earlier. Suddenly a white Prius, driven by a fetching blond woman wearing aviators, pulled alongside.

"Are you Dallas Smith?" she asked.

To a road hermit, here was a vision in blond hair and sunglasses. I didn't know her. She pulled into the parking lot beside me. It was Lana Sain, the woman along with Mark Yother, who'd run briefly with me in the Cookeville race a few months earlier.

"You mind if I make your picture?" she'd asked.

I stood while she made the photo—which she then posted on social media. For some reason, I failed to make hers.

This is a town of multiple memories. A short time after Lana left me that day, my stone-injured foot did a very strange thing. I'd been limping on it for the best part of two days and I didn't know if it was going to hold up. I feared a fracture. I was approaching what I thought was an Arby's and I wanted a roast beef sandwich. Just then, the foot snapped and gave way. It was like a catastrophic break. I nearly hit the ground. I managed to stay upright, and hobbled a few steps into the restaurant where I could sit down, a sudden need greater than food. The restaurant wasn't an Arby's, but instead a Hardees—or something. My mind was broken, too.

I bought a burger and fries and a strawberry milkshake and ate while the foot rested. From the burger place, I hobbled a short ways to a hotel and got a room. I set my alarm for three o'clock next morning. I didn't expect to be able to stand. After six hours of sleep I got up. The foot was completely healed. There was no trace of the aggravation it had caused me for two days or of the apparent catastrophic break a few hours earlier. It was healed. How the foot accomplished that miracle remains a complete mystery.

Now, two years later I trudged along the same sidewalk again, and I knew I was not going to be so lucky. The shredded soles on my feet where not going to suddenly repair themselves.

You run solo because you want to, eschewing whatever strength companionship might bring. You want to practice the power to go inside and find the strength there to deal with the pain, the bone-weary need to keep going. At times it approaches a lonely solitude. Those times are countered by memories that come around like ghosts: Runners like Jameelah, Sergio and Don; visitors like Marie, Ella, Tom Silver, Mark Yother and Lana Sain; Road Angels like Kim Nutt, and, yes, even a nameless Mexican laborer—all of them, they crowd in. They defeat the loneliness. Your solo strength is an illusion. You'd had help all along. You'd denied it. I trudge along brooding.

Suddenly, a car turned into the parking lot and came toward me. It was a white car, a white Prius. As the car stopped, I knew who it was.

"I work up on the mountain, and I was afraid I would get home too late to see you," Lana Sain said.

But no, I'm not so fast. I was still out picking my way toward a hotel. Lana had food and water in her car, but I didn't need anything.

"How about a bandana? she asked.

"What for?"

"Put it around your neck. You can wet it and it'll be cool."

"She poured cold water on a blue bandana and I pulled it tight against my cooked neck. She was right. It was cool and pleasant. We stood there. I remembered to turn the tables on the young woman who had surprised me—astonished me!—two years earlier and even made a picture for social media. Yes, on her I now turned the tables.

"Can I make a picture?" I asked her.

We faced the sun. This time she was wearing white Oakleys. She pushed them on top of her blond hair and we leaned together for a selfie. In the photo I look much happier than you'd think a man with my burning soles could.

Twice now, Lana has surprised me and, in so doing, achieved permanence in my mental ledgers of running. This day had been one of extraordinary meetings.

I trudged on toward the hotel I knew I'll find at the Interstate and came to a market. It was time to grab some milk for supper and breakfast and to fetch my standard supper, Beanee Weenees. Don's advice nagged me and so I checked. To my great surprise, there sat several bottles of hydrogen peroxide.

Once I got into a room at the hotel, I followed the veteran's advice. I ran an inch of water into the plastic waste basket, poured in an undetermined amount of peroxide and soaked each foot.

"How big's your foot?" Don had asked. It just fit the wastebasket. It was Wednesday, day seven. In a few hours I'd put my shoes back on, and they would not come off again until Friday night. I set my alarm for one thirty and went to bed.

Chapter Eight

Burning Soles

It would be a big day. Or, it would not. It is forty-eight miles to Kimball, where you can find the next hotel.

The road I run on is dark and asleep. The first thing it did this morning when I set out on it was to cross the Interstate, I-24, a road that never sleeps. That was at two-thirty. Now I trot along in the dark, worried, as always, whether I'm on the right course.

The Interstate noise fades and then transforms in a worrisome way that adds to my anxiety: it appears to come from the wrong direction. My course, U.S. 41, and I-24 both head south, gradually diverging. I-24 is to my right, but for some reason its noise seems to come from the left. Maybe terrain or atmospheric conditions cause that phenomenon. It makes me careful to confirm Arnold Center Road teeing in from the south. As a rational fact, I'm on course.

It's called the Hillsboro Highway, which is maybe more appealing than the name U.S. 41. By either name, it goes through the hamlet of Hillsboro. And when after a couple of hours I get there, it is still dark. But Hillsboro is waking up and there is a market open already. I see a cop sitting in his car across the road from the market. I trot up to his window and bend down,

"You got any idea how far it is to Pelham?" I ask.

"It's a good ways." That doesn't tell me much.

"That's the next little town. I was just wondering. My maps don't show Pelham very well."

"It's a good ways."

"In that case, I guess I'd better get some water here while I can then."

"Yeah, it's a good ways."

"Thanks a bunch."

I reckon you could say I got the idea that it was a good ways to Pelham. So, I hit the mart for a bottle of water and wander on. In a while the sky lightens and the horizon emerges. The long ridge in front of me is the Cumberland Plateau. I'm going to climb up on it. But it's miles away yet, "a good ways" yet. I'll trot toward it a few hours. The sun ball slips above the ridge and then seems to park itself there for my amusement. At that moment I'm passing a farm pond close to the road. The sky is reflecting in it. I could call it a frog pond, because a bullfrog in it is grunting like old grandfather, deep and mellow.

It is enough to stop me. I pull out my phone and make a photo that will become my favorite of the trip. In it you see the sunrise, the pond's reflected sky and the plateau with a long fog bank hugging its flank. You can almost hear the bullfrog's hoarse croaking.

It is going to be another hot day. My feet are no better. I hope the danger of infection is lessened by the peroxide bath I gave them last night. I stop in the shade of a pine to report my position to Carl Laniak and simply type "Dallas, 264." He answers back, "Alright!"

So, I started at mile 252 and nearly five hours later I've traveled just twelve miles, to 264. It is amazing and disgusting at the same time. I've done mostly walking, but at least a little bit of running. Yet, I've come just twelve miles. The two-miles-an-hour principle is slipping into play. I don't care. I'll do what I can, though enfeebled I may become. My personality won't change. Whatever happens to my body, the essential *self* of myself will endure. I'll still be here, ya'll, and I'll be myself, too.

One in a situation so desperate should do what? Make humorous pictures, of course. The sun stretches my shadow across Hillsboro Highway. I hold my camera as I trot along and make a picture of it and post it on social media with the caption, appropriately enough, "Hillsboro Highway." The great stretched shadow reminds me of Plastic Man. Why have we not yet had a blockbuster Plastic Man movie?

Thigh-high chicory decorated by showy blue flowers hangs over the pavement edge. Each blossom radiates the brightest blue. I make a picture of that, too and write the caption: "My bright blue smile is yours, all yours." By which, of course, I mean it is mine. Because I am the one who is here, and I'm the one who has paid the cost to be here.

Pelham is a crossroads. Harry and Ollie have set out

a table of food and drinks, all covered by a picnic cano-py. They maintain a campground and country market and used to have a restaurant as well. Vol State runners would stop in for food. Though they no longer have the restaurant, they are still friends to runners. I have a pack of crackers, a soft drink and refill my bottles, leave some money and head on, avoiding the temptation to stretch out in the shade.

It's no good. A few miles later I realize I'm in a situa-tion I've never been in before, one compounded to double jeopardy: I've grown profoundly weak and profoundly sleepy, both worse than I've ever known. I waited seven-ty-five years to say that. I trod on this road before with-out this trouble. What is wrong? Forget running, even my walk is halting and feeble now. I can find no place for a nap. I know not to lie down in the road. The smooth pave-ment seems so softly inviting...

So desperate am I, that I walk in on a carport of a country house. Two vehicles are parked on it. Maybe I can take a nap on the concrete. Through the screen door I can hear a washing machine running, but no one answers my knock. I walk around to the front door and try again. Still, there is no answer. No choice but to head back on the road, which I do. At that moment, coming from the house, I hear an outraged watchdog raising hell. His turf was invaded and he slept through it. The best barking opportunity ever and he missed it. Now he's mad about it. Incompetent mutt. If I'd stretched out on the carport, he might've eaten my face off, I think in rueful but thankful irony.

I'm running on raw nubs. Add my burning soles

to my problems and I'm in, not double but instead, triple jeopardy. My feet have never been in such shredded shape. Unprecedented conditions piling on when just one would be a threat. Decisions I've made and not made in this run have brought me to this particular place in this particular condition, here, in this road, now. Who else can I blame?

All morning I've passed through a near-flat agricultural landscape of pastures, of fields in corn and soybeans. That is about to change. The Cumberland Plateau looms ahead like a bulwark, its wooded slope steep-faced and imposing. It raises its boulders and bluffs and oaks like a forbidding wall you cannot scale. The road disappears at its foot, swallowed by its green density, swallowed by its spreading immensity. That's the edge I have to touch, to touch and climb.

Instead, I turn and look behind me. What I see suggests a movie scene. The road stretches across the tableland to a shimmering vanishing point. Just this side of hazy nothingness, I can make out a lone figure on the road, a dark, ant-sized but upright pedestrian, one flopping and flapping, loose jointed and over-laden, a prehistoric caveman wearing skins and burned black by the sun, one slowly gaining size on my retina.

My eyes gaze vaguely. It can only be Sergio. He approaches, running, alone now, as he was when last I saw him some three days ago, when I left him waiting for Lynda in Hampshire. Yes, it was three days ago. Lynda has dropped to the crewed category now. Sergio runs alone, as do I. He jogs up and stops.

"It doesn't hurt as much if I run," he says.

"I can't run. All I can do is look for a place to sleep," I reply.

"When does the road head up the mountain?" He catches my glance and we both look at where the road vanishes ahead as if swallowed by a cave.

"I think you're looking at it." We chat a little bit more, but Sergio is on a mission. He starts running toward the mountain.

Then turning, half stopping, "Come on!" he says.

"I can't, man."

The road makes a hard left and enters the trees. An observer in Pelham with super vision would finally see me disappear, just as Sergio did, just as the road does. The road and I climb through the trees for the next three miles, getting over the plateau's edge. I look for a place to sleep the whole way. There is no place.

Perhaps, I should stop on the top in Monteagle. There's a hotel there. It's a short ways off the course. Monteagle is forty miles from the finish line, an easily managed stretch if I were well rested. I could hole up there and get well-rested. I've held the plan in the back of my mind a couple of days. The rap against holing up there is that I did not have to stop there on my run two years ago. I hate making concessions.

Near the top comes a gap in the trees due to a powerline right-of-way. I can gaze back on the pastoral land toward Pelham. I tweet a picture. Lana Sain, soon comes back with an answering tweet, something like: "@smithbend is already in Monteagle! Amazing!" It is a great deal less amazing if you know I left Manchester at two thirty this morning.

The decision point is now. In Monteagle, the course veers sharply left, while the road to the hotel angles right. Perhaps one should hold a moment of serious debate. If it happens, a disinterested observer would not notice it: I continue doggedly on course. Monteagle has a linear city park. It is little more than a grassy strip between two roads. But a concrete walk runs the length of it and there are small scattered trees and an occasional bench. I drop my pack at one of the benches. I can't go on. I have to sleep. I set my phone to chime in fifteen minutes and go to sleep.

The sleep is not long enough, but I get up and go. Tracy City is just six miles further. I pass a Monteagle house where my son and his family lived for a while, make a picture and text it to him. This run has extracurricular memories.

The winding and rolling two-lane to Tracy City is one of the most dangerous stretches of the run. Traffic is continual. Only a narrow strip of pavement extends past the fog line for escape. Its width is mostly taken by the rumble strip and overhanging weeds.

A country church on the right is a place to get water. I know that from my first run. I stopped here for water then. There's a foundation faucet. As I walked toward the faucet that time, I saw a truck pull into a drive down the hill, and a man got out. It was a church deacon, I figured, and he was going to check me out. I passed the corner and was filling a bottle when the man came around the corner. It was Joshua Holmes. He'd already finished the race and was driving along the course checking on runners.

That was a surprise. I asked Josh about Diane Bolton, she of the "poor dallas" fame. I'd not seen her since Shelbyville and wondered where she was.

"She's about ready to go over the edge," he told me.

Vol State runners have to climb over one edge of the plateau and down the other edge. Diane was nearly to Jasper, probably fifteen miles ahead of me.

Now two years later: The sidewalk in Tracy City passes under a giant oak shade tree just before ending at a parking lot for an exercise place. That's where I drop my pack again for another nap. It is a brief nap like in Monteagle. As I am getting up, a girl in yoga pants gets out of her car, glances at the rising vagrant and dashes into the gym.

Sometimes a fifteen-minute nap can be refreshing. Today, not so. I continue on as sleepy as before. My discipline is deserting me and I'm only vaguely aware of it. I had a snack in Pelham around breakfast time. In Monteagle I failed to get any lunch, although there were restaurants. Now, in Tracy City that trend continues, and I walk past a restaurant. Going deep into calorie debt should alarm me. The alarm can't penetrate my sleepy mind.

A market is the best I can do. I stop for an ice cream, which I promptly eat. I take a sausage-like meat stick called a Slim Jim and a pack of peanuts with me. It's not much but it's all I want. All I want? It's all my diminished mind even thinks I need. I trundle on down the street.

A man on foot catches me from behind, asking if I'm who I am. And, yes, I admit it. He's been watching for me. He manages the auto parts store I've just passed, he says.

He has read one of my books and he knows one of my running friends. He just wanted to meet me.

The runner he now sees standing before him is likely not the one he pictured from reading the book. It must be a disappointment. The one in the book was never in the shape of this one. I whine about how bad I feel and about how I have to find a place to sleep. There are no hotels in Tracy City.

"You might be able to sleep on one of the picnic tables at Foster Falls."

"How far is that?"

"It's about eight miles."

Eight miles, not even a long morning jog, but it's a long ways for me now. I can't tell him that. My lizard brain vainly holds onto lizard pride. I try to be amicable. I hope I am.

How can I even tell him about Foster Falls? I slept on one of those picnic tables once. It was a long time ago, the only time I was there. Now that ghost comes back. How'd I happen to sleep in that place?

I'd parked my truck in Tracy City, and headed out on a solo hike of the Fiery Gizzard Trail, a picturesque hike through Grundy State Forest alongside Fiery Gizzard Creek. On an excursion from the creek, I climbed up to the top and walked out on the ultimate edge of a point jutting out in space like the prow of a ship. Far below, the green hills rolled away like waves. There was a stunted pine sapling beside me clinging to that bare ledge, somehow finding enough soil in the seams between layers of naked sandstone to make a stingy living. It reached a limb into the yawning space. I took ahold of it and leaned far out over the swooping void. I made a foamy ball of spit and let it drop. I hung onto the scrawny limb and watched. It fell straight, glowing in the sun like a point of falling light. Then it began to curve as currents swept it underneath me, and blinked out when it entered the bluff's shadow.

I was wearing a tee shirt and didn't even take a jacket or a day pack that day. That's how a greenhorn does it. My all-day walk ended at Foster Falls. My son Rory, when he lived in Monteagle, was manager of a mine at Sherwood, Tennessee, south of Foster Falls, near the Alabama-Tennessee state line. The plan was for him to swing by Foster Falls after work and pick me up.

That plan won't bear careful examination. I reached Foster Falls that afternoon before his schedule permitted him to get there. I had to wait. That's what picnic tables are for. I remember being cold, trying to sleep, and I needed the jacket I didn't take. That's how a greenhorn does it all right. It finally worked out, and Rory found me there. The hike wasn't perfect but it nearly was. According to *Backpacker Magazine*, which I was subscribing to in those days, that walk is one of the best in Tennessee, or even in the U.S.A. I'm lucky I took it. I haven't been back to Foster Falls. Until now I'd never connected it to Vol State.

After leaving the enthused gentleman from the parts store, I wander on through Tracy City. I come to a church that has a small wooden deck in the shade on its eastern side. I climb the steps. The little deck is where they store their mops and buckets. It's suitable. I shuck my pack and sit on the deck resting my feet on the top step. I dine on the

Slim Jim and peanuts. That's supper.

Day eight doesn't end until seven-thirty tomorrow morning. My goal has been to reach The Rock by then, finish under eight days. That dream is dead and buried here in Tracy City. I feel like I've wasted the day. The appalling condition of my feet, my plunging energy level, the need to sleep, they've all gathered here, a grand intersection of catastrophes. I've hit a bad patch in Tracy City.

The nearest hotel ahead is hours away. This deck is my hotel. My plan is to nap an hour. That will be my sleep. I'm leaving my shoes on. Then I'll soldier on through the night. It is a long lonely stretch across the Cumberland Plateau to Jasper.

I make a pillow of my pack and rest my head. I close my eyes and wait for oblivion. The fading day hums and murmurs a soft question like a restless wind's gentle stirring:

Let me see if I have this straight? You barely have the energy to walk, you can't hold your eyes open and your feet are so raw it'll takes weeks to grow new soles, you just ate peanuts and a stick of grease for supper, and after a nap you're going to walk across the Cumberland Plateau in the dark of night. Is that it?

Oblivion answers.

Chapter Nine

Scorpio's Stinger

This two-lane cuts south across the plateau toward Scorpio's stinger. The Scorpion hovers low there in the southern sky, its stinger curled and ready to strike a hard land. The sky is dark this night, the moon absent, on the other side of the globe. The air is clear and stars glitter on the black dome overhead, their puny light offering me scarcely more than token help. Trees crowd in. I hold fast to the fog line with the bright oval made by my hand-held light, my main tether to the physical world.

I am walking, but only at a plodding pace, a walk punctuated on occasion by side lurches, staggers and missteps. I have to be especially careful when a vehicle passes. Otherwise, I keep my head down and hold the fog line in the glowing circle that my light makes. I can't run.

I can't run. I'm yet in the eighth day of my run. And I can't run. So, I walk. The front soles of my feet have delaminated into separate, tattered layers oozing a slimy soup. Each toe suffers a similar condition, just on a smaller scale. Several days of triple-digit heat have damaged my feet to an extent I haven't seen before. Each step is painful. I can walk with pain. Anyone can. But I can't run, pain or not.

This highway stretches from Tracy City, the place I've left, to Jasper, the place where I'm trying to go. There's no hotel in Jasper. If I get there, it's only five more miles to Kimball, where there is a hotel. If I should make it to Jasper, maybe I can make it on to Kimball. But I don't know that. My ability to travel is diminished, severely so.

There were cars and trailer trucks on the road before dark, but now, deep into the night, only an occasional vehicle passes. That's the totality of good news I know.

Trailer trucks are what I dread. Getting out of their way is a problem. The pavement past the fog line is no wider than a couch cushion. The rumble strip takes half of that. Overhanging weeds and grass cover the remainder. The strip's scooped cut-outs, regularly spaced, must be an inch deep. I've inspected their arrangement in some detail. Stepping on it makes hurting feet hurt harder and improves the chance of stumbling into a truck's path. The rumble strip is sorely in my way.

When the truck comes, I trudge across the rumble strip and press up against the weeds. There won't be much clearance. If I don't stop walking, I may stumble. I stop, facing away, legs spread, and bend over, bracing my hands on my knees like you've seen tired basketball players do, and wait for the truck to either blow by or blast me into infinity. Only an occasional truck punctuates the night now. Mostly it's just cars now and not so many of them anymore.

I trudge on through the night, following U.S. 41 south.

Back home, I have an old friend. Sometimes he walks on the track while I'm running on it. His walk is slow, really, painfully slow. I pass him time and time again. He walks like someone recovering from surgery in the hall of the hospital, shuffling, as in dense sludge. He's walked that way since I've known him. I've wondered why he didn't walk faster. But now that I'm walking the same way I understand better. I have no ability to walk faster. And running is a hopeless lost dream. Like my old friend, I suppose it's a matter of energy. But I don't know medicine. Maybe an endrocrinologist would explain my condition in term of hormones, but I don't know that either. I know less with each passing hour.

I have to get to Jasper. If I dare to hope, from there it's five more miles to Kimball. Then we're talking fourteen more miles to the end of the race, on Sand Mountain. Where am I now? I don't know, maybe eight miles from Jasper, say; plus five more, then add the last fourteen. That makes twenty-seven miles to go. That's what's left of the 314 miles I had at the start. Twenty-seven is barely more than a marathon, which I can do in less than four hours— under normal conditions. Twenty-seven seems a distance too large now to contemplate. It is odd to consider that the longest of distances would, in the end, come down to strategies for the shortest of distances.

First, I have to get to Jasper. There'll be food and water there. Then we'll see.

I don't know what will happen to my feet. They are shredded. Two years ago, a runner eventually lost his leg due to an infection from this run, I've heard. I know the danger. Don Winkley, the veteran, warned me convincingly a day ago—or was it two? Whatever it was it was before the last night I slept in a bed. And so, scared, I soaked them in peroxide and water like he'd said. What I remember best is how my feet were raw enough that they'd stick to the tile floor like raw slabs of meat. After a brief sleep that night I donned my shoes and left out of that hotel. I haven't had my shoes off since then. My feet don't keep me from walking. They just make it painful.

I trudge on through the night, my feet worrying me. But they're not even the worst problem I have. Sleep is. I have to find a place for a nap. There's no doubt. But there's no place. My flashlight shows me. Trees, weeds and brush line the road. My feet have never been in such sad shape, and I've never been so sleepy, both. It's late but I'm still in day eight, same as I was when I passed through Pelham, the place the cop thought was a good ways from Hillsboro. Still in day eight, can that be right? The climb up Monteagle Mountain was no more than a fruitless three-mile search for a place to nap, a search that didn't end until I found the park walk in the town of Monteagle. The fifteen-minute nap there didn't help like a nap should, nor did the fifteen-minute nap six miles later in Tracy City. Nap after nap, and I could not catch up. Still can't.

All the naps accomplished only one thing: they put me behind schedule. So that, when at Tracy City I'd decided to trudge on through the night, I though a substantial rest was needed, which the one-hour sleep on the church deck was. I thought it was. But when I headed south, I soon found that it hadn't helped much either. Soon, I was in the night I'd looked forward to. I was as sleepy in nighttime as in daytime.

Night would be cooler, and so I thought I'd be able to manage a measure of running. Maybe that would wake me up. I soon realized running was impossible. Now I walk, inching my way across the Cumberland Plateau. But sleep is all I can think about, hour after hour, until I nearly fall down. An unwelcome thought haunts me: lie down on the narrow space between the fog line and weeds. Crazy, of course, a truck might squash me, but the need for sleep is so strong, reason makes no sense. I manage to trudge on.

Foster Falls becomes the focus of my being. I can sleep there, like the man in Tracy City said. There'll be picnic tables. A picnic table to stretch out on, what an impossible luxury! I must find that picnic table. Somewhere ahead, somewhere toward Scorpio's stinger, somewhere south, somewhere...

The night holds nothing anymore. I don't care about Scorpio's stinger. I don't care about the stars. I hardly look at them. To hell with their happy twinkle. The road goes south, and I go south. The fog line, the rumble-strip notches pass through the circle my light makes on the road. Mostly, I keep my head down. Occasionally, I shine my light around to search for a smooth surface I can sleep on. There's no place, just weeds, brush, trees, and the tempting strip between fog line and weeds.

I raise my light and there's a sign. Foster Falls, it says. I've come to Foster Falls. It has taken me over three hours to cover the eight miles. I no longer even think that's worse than just walking. I don't care. A drive leads to the right, and I start down it. There are houses spaced along the drive. Or they could be park buildings, maybe a mixture of park buildings and houses. No, houses, I think. In the dark I can't be certain. I walk down the drive looking for a place to sleep. A driveway is not safe. A car might run me over. Someone's front yard might raise an alarm, a dog. I keep walking. Soon, I realize the problem with Foster Falls—it is too far off the main road. I'll waste too much time if I keep going down this drive looking for the promised picnic tables.

I haven't found Foster Falls, only the road to it. So, I reverse course. No luck here. On the way back out, just before I come to the main road again, there is a yard— mowed anyway—on the left. A building beyond could be a park building or house. A spot of bare ground appears in my light. It's a place where the soil is too poor to grow even weeds. I stretch out on it, my pack for a pillow, as usual. Soon, I realize I've chosen an impossible bed. Bugs and ants begin crawling on my skin. After fifteen minutes I have to get up. And trudge on.

Back on the main road, I'm headed south again, as sleepy as ever. Relief seems impossible. This seems a place I can't be in and yet can't escape. I can do nothing but trudge on, pressing the weeds to make way for the occasional car or truck. Their passing punctuates the night, a blast rupturing tranquility, a roar receding, and then lonely silence again. I drift on through the darkest night.

A light is shining in my face. It's on a guy's head. It's a runner wearing a headlamp. He leans on two hiking poles and stands looking at me. I can almost reach out and touch him.

"I didn't see you," I say.

"You didn't see me?" he chuckles, "he-he-he."

No wonder he's incredulous. Who could believe that statement? He'd been standing, watching me approach. I wasn't seeing anything. I just shrug it off. We walk on together, sharing tales of our misery. His name is Fred Davis. I'd not met him before now.

Fred is like me. He's whipped. I move to the right-hand lane to give him room. He lives in Cleveland, Ohio, he tells me. He tells me things about his life there. He has to help his mom. She is getting on in years and she doesn't always agree with him. I can appreciate his helping his mom. He's a good son. My mom and dad are both gone. I had to help them. It wasn't easy. Fred and I pass the time drifting south.

"I was walking the wrong way," Fred says. He'd gotten turned around and had been going toward Tracy City. Then he came to a place he knew he'd seen before and turned around again. I guess he doesn't know the stars. Now he's going the right way. I can't say much of anything, except for how sleepy I am. But I tell him that over and over.

"I can't walk straight," Fred says, wearing his headlight beside me. He says it as a simple fact, like I might say I can't sing. "I keep curving to the left. Then I run into the weeds."

I don't know the cure for that. What he says is true though. He gradually curves left until he stumbles across the rumble strip and then into the weeds. He stops and looks around, as if mildly surprised. I watch as he resets, gets back to the center of the lane and starts out again. Soon, though, he drifts closer and closer to the left edge again and then repeats the whole process over. I don't try to warn him when he heads to the weeds. It's his routine. I reckon he's used to it. Better to not interfere.

"You're the opposite of me, you curve to the right," Fred says to me. I don't think that's correct. I did go right to occupy the right lane, but I haven't run into the weeds. We each have a lane, now that the road is deserted. I join Fred in single file whenever a car comes along. Other than that I like the right lane. My light keeps searching for a place to lie down—or I may fall down. I wish I could talk to Fred. I like talking. But I know I'm not good company, mostly whining about sleep.

I can see a pale glow low in the southern sky. "That's Jasper," I say wearily. The information scarcely interests either one of us. Jasper is still too far off. The thought fades with barely a stir.

We come to a driveway. It's on Fred's side. Only it's not a driveway. It only goes ten feet. The road builders made the start of a driveway to maybe a planned house or barn. But the short segment was never connected to a longer drive. It's a driveway to nowhere. It's a bed. I kick aside some of the scattered gravel on it and drop my pack.

"I'm going to take a nap."

"What? Right here? But...I don't think it's safe," Fred says. My feet will be close to the traffic, but out of the traffic by three or four feet.

"It'll be all right."

My pack is especially made for ultrarunners. Actually, I use two, a waist pack that holds one water bottle and a backpack that holds two. Besides bottles, there's not much else. Bottles empty, the whole business weighs just four pounds. I drop both packs. Fred still hesitates. He wants to dissuade me. He thinks it's too dangerous, but finally he drifts on. I'm alone again.

The temperature has fallen into the sixties, I know. I need more than just shorts and tee. I do have a windbreaker in my pack, a thin filmy thing. I put it on. And I have an emergency poncho, the kind folded up to the size of a folded bandana. I unfold it. It would help retain a little body warmth. The thin clingy plastic tangles in the dark. I can't untangle it or find the openings. I tug and pull and finally give up. I wrap the tangled wad around my bare legs and rest my head on my pack. I lie in the driveway to nowhere, my feet pointed to the traffic.

Then Fred yells from somewhere down the road.

"Hey Dallas, here's a better place!"

It's the parking lot of an abandoned business, or some such. Fred is worried about me. That's touching but I'm desperate for sleep and already settled in.

"That's okay, Fred, thanks, but I'm okay here," I yell back. After that, Fred is quiet. I reckon he drifts on toward Jasper. My eyes are closed and I start to drift off.

A car stops at my feet. It sets there idling. I open my eyes. I can see the tail light. The car is headed south but sitting in the northbound lane, sitting at my feet. The night is black but the tail light is bright. I wait, not stirring.

Finally, a man's voice comes out of the dark.

"Sir, are you all right?"

"Yes sir, I'm fine. I just need to take a nap. Thanks."
The car pulls away, toward Jasper and I fall asleep.

I wake up cold. My watch shows I've been asleep
an hour. I remember none of it. How many trailer trucks
blasted past my extended legs, I don't know. How many
cars, I don't know. I remember nothing. But now I'm cold.
In a run plagued by intense heat, ironically, I'm cold. I
can't sleep when I'm cold. So, I have to go. I unwind the
plastic from my legs, wad it and stuff it in my pack. I head
down the road, toward the sky glow once more, toward
where I trust Jasper spreads, beaming its photons into the
dark summer night. It is as before, feet painful as before,
sleepy as before. There is no help for it. It seems I've been
doing this forever and that I'm doomed to keep doing it
forevermore.

It may be wishful thinking or it may be my imagination,
but it seems the sky glow is growing, that I might be getting
closer. I can begin to sense the plateau drop-off, where the
road begins its descent into the Sequatchie Valley and into
Jasper—sense it more than actually see it. A car passes
going in that direction and I watch its tail lights until it
goes out of sight, hoping to see it go over the edge. The
observation is inconclusive—there are gentle rollers and
slight curves. So, I can't tell why the car's lights eventually
disappear.

When I do start downhill the sky gets bigger. The
change in slope brings no relief, just dull acknowledgment.
Going downhill on my raw feet is no easier and I'm as

sleepy as ever. The descent is three miles long and I know it's merely the next thing I have to do. The road winds downward, unrelentingly down, elevation monotonically decreasing, a mathematician would say. No possibility of lying down anywhere, or even of sitting down. On my left a raw rock bluff rises steeply into the trees, barely any roadway shoulder at all, even less space for an escape lane than up on top. On my right a guard rail crowds tight against the pavement and past the rail the hill drops sharply through rocks and trees. At least one runner driven crazy for sleep will cross that rail, braving the snakes, rocks and poison ivy. But not this runner. I know too well what's down there.

It's almost claustrophobic, this segment. Trees overhand the guard rail, and trees clinging to the bluff overhead reach outward blocking most of the already puny starlight from reaching the road. It's dark. Stars are faint help. I'm not sure I could even see the fog line well enough to follow it without my flashlight. And so, I lose even that small comfort. My light begins to go out. Batteries are going. I've seen this before. The light will fade fast. That must be a characteristic of an LED. I know I have to act fast, while I still have some light left.

I hunker down on the fog line. If a vehicle comes now, I barely have room to get out of the lane. I dig my last two batteries out of my pack using the last of my fading light. The next step has to be done in the dark, by feel alone. If I drop something I'll have hell trying to find it. I screw the top off the light and dump out the two spent batteries, being very careful to notice their polarity by the bump on the positive end of the batteries. Now, I drop in the fresh batteries and screw the head back on. Twist it tight, which is the "on" switch. Except this time it doesn't come on. I've had trouble with it before. Cussing does not help. I whack it hard against the palm of my hand. It flashes—blip!— suddenly, with near startling brightness, and stays on. I resolve to make sure I don't risk turning it off. My trudge continues. My circle of light slides along the fog line. That's all you'd see. There is nothing else in my world.

How long, how long does it take to get down this mountain? A car comes up the hill and stops. It's Jan in her van, Meat Wagon, looking for fresh meat. She is ready to pick up runners injured or otherwise ready to quit. Actually, she wants you to succeed, but she'll help you if you don't. It's strictly a volunteer service. She's devoted, patrolling at midnight. She loses sleep, too. She ran the race herself two years ago and so knows what the runners go through. So moved was she that she has come back the last two years to help. She has a knack for showing up at my weakest moments.

I describe in whining detail just how bad my situation is, the sleep deprivation, the painful feet. But I don't step into the van. I remember that that act would end my adventure as an unsupported runner, even if I didn't ride but only rested. Vehicles are off limits. Stepping into one, I'd be out of luck, permitted to continue on as a supported or crewed runner, albeit one without an actual crew.

Her van sitting in the dark road, Jan listens while I talk through the open window about how I need to rest.

"There's a church at the bottom of the hill," she offers.

"Maybe you can find a place to sit down there."

"I hope I can find it. Maybe I'll find it." I'm not very sure about anything anymore. Jan is sympathetic. But she can't help until I declare failure. Then I could rest in her van. I could sleep in her van. I want to sleep. But I'm still not ready to give up. Jan drives on.

What is there to say about this?—about the raw feet, about energy crashed to a plodding level, about multi-day sleep deprivation?—all conditions self-inflicted. What do I think about it? This: it's no big deal. There are people in the world with worse hurts that didn't choose them. They are entitled to complain. I am not. I made mistakes. The mistakes were mine alone. They've brought me to this dark place.

What would you ask me? What was it Jan said when she drove up just now? Something like, "Are you all right?" A simple question, but the long answer is complicated. Short answer: I'll be better once I find a place to rest where I won't be run over. I don't see me ever writing about this. Who would want to read misery? Who would want to write it?

After an hour of plodding downhill, I come to Jasper. The first indication you've entered town is a Seventh-day Adventist Church, a brick building on the left, the church Jan was talking about, I reckon. Boulders line the front yard to keep cars off the grass. I could sit on one, "sit" being the word Jan used. But I need more than sitting. I need a prone position. I circle around behind the building. Here I find a covered concrete patio and a back door. A rubber door mat spreads itself in front of the door. That's my bed. Nobody will find me here unless he's prowling the night. I throw my pack off and once again wrap the tangled emergency rain coat around my legs. It's one-thirty as I stretch out on the door mat. I remember that and nothing more.

Chapter Ten

Party Hardy

I wake up from a total blackout, one lacking sounds in the night, dreams or any other disturbance that I can recall. Oblivion reigned for four hours. It's five-thirty and I need to pee. That's not a problem. Nobody is around. I simply walk to the back edge of the lawn where the bushes start.

I have a Snickers I've been carrying around and I dig it out for breakfast. So much for that. Four hours of sleep. Time to go. It is nineteen miles to the finish, to The Rock, THE ROCK! If I only make two miles per hour, I should get there by mid-afternoon, later if I go slower.

I have to work my way through Jasper. Last time, two years ago, it was hard. I went through late at night in the dark and there was heavy traffic. Some stretches had no sidewalk and no shoulder, just a ditch, which, in the dark, I couldn't see very well. One runner broke his ankle and had to drop out just nineteen miles from the finish, after coming all this way. His luck was bad. Falling into the ditch could break my ankle too. Myself, there were times, I'd stand in a driveway and wait for oncoming traffic to let up and then rush down to the next driveway where I could get out of traffic and wait again. It was dangerous. I felt invisible in the approaching bright lights. I didn't want to go through town in the dark again.

Friend Diane Taylor was bitten by a dog here. She had no chance to catch the animal or talk to its owner. She called a doctor friend, John Spencer, who told her how to do first aid on the wound, and he told her she'd just have to assume that the dog didn't have rabies. Small comfort. An owner that lets his dog run free to bite people also may be irresponsible enough to ignore the dog's rabies shots. Left untreated, the fatality rate of rabies for humans is near one hundred percent. She had to wait it out. Lucky for her the rabies didn't develop.

Another runner went through Jasper that year wearing a white long-sleeved dress shirt he'd bought at Wal-Mart, a cheap shirt. That's what he likes to run in. He doesn't have to be frugal. The shirt is his style statement. If he were younger you'd call him a hipster runner. The cops thought he was a crook. They gave him the treatment, surrounded him, one in front one in back, intimidated him pretty good. There was nothing racial in the event. All three men were white. After the race, he called the police department and arranged a meeting with the two cops at the station. Then he gave them the treatment. He's an older gentleman. He told them he was "quite wealthy," which is quite true, I reckon, and which also had the effect of signifying that he could sue *their* shirts off. He's not only wealthy but also tough. The two cops learned a lesson about picking on old guys in white shirts.

Despite these incidents, Jasper is not an evil place, but, I think, rather a friendly one. These events could have happened at almost any place. A friendly gentleman named Steve Smalling from here did me a very great honor and helped me, too, in that race two years ago. He'd driven his car to down past Kimball and was handing out cold bottles of water to runners there. That's where I found him this same morning two years ago. He gave me two bottles of water. He also gave me his card and asked me to send him an e-mail once I got back home. Although it had gotten wet with sweat and dog-eared from wear, I still had the card when I got back to my Cookeville home. So, I sent him an email. He interviewed me and made my experience the major part of a vivid story he wrote in the magazine of the Chattanooga Track Club. So, I'll judge Jasper from Steve Smalling's altruism, not from the other unfortunate incidents that took place here two years ago.

This year as I trudge through Jasper—in morning light this time—I remember Steve, and I recall that he posted a day or so ago on Facebook that he was setting a cooler full of bottled water in his front yard, that he was going to be there, too, to welcome runners, except for some chore that would take him away for a while.

"Help yourself to the water regardless," he advised. I shuffle along wondering which yard is Steve's and looking for his Road Angel aid station. But, alas, never spy it.

Johnny Adams catches me. What the hell!

"Johnny, what're you doing back here? I figured you

were way out in front. I thought you would've finished by now."

Ah, but there are many stories on this road. He'd gotten sick and had to hole up for a day until he was able to go on. So, here he is back here with a hack. But not entirely. His walk is spritely, and I'm still shuffling like last night, a pokey plod. I let him go on.

"You look strong now. Good luck, man," I say, the usual banal runner talk.

It takes a while to get through Jasper. I ought to stop for some food, but I'm waiting until a market on the far side of town. After a while Johnny passes me again, surprising me once more.

"I stopped for some breakfast," he says.

I didn't even see the restaurant. Somehow, I keep doing everything wrong. Little wonder I have no energy. I've had practically no food since the Slim Jim and peanuts back in Tracy City yesterday and the candy bar this morning. Johnny marches away again.

The Jasper Quick Stop is the market I've been watching for, an Exxon station. I remember it from two years ago—Jasper seems full of memories. Two years ago I went into the store around nine o'clock. A middle-aged woman, dressed in finery that seemed out of place in the convenience store, stood in line for the cashier. She asked, so I told her where I'd come from and where I was going. Her mouth fell open. It wasn't disbelief. She believed me. I couldn't tell if her expression was one of fawning admiration or morbid fascination. Her eyes sparkled. I remember the pleats in her off-white skirt, how easily they draped.

I can get some Gatorade and candy bars here. A lone man, well fed and well dressed, is pumping gasoline into his SUV as I walk across the apron. He looks up and greets me with a smile and a wave. I veer from my course toward the store and walk up to him. I don't know why. It's just good to talk sometimes. He knows what I'm up to. He's not a runner but he knows a man who is, a man in his church. And he tells me about him. I begin to get a hunch.

"It's not Steve Smalling, is it?"

"Oh! You know Steve!" It surprises him—a random man from who knows where comes slouching through your town and he knows one of your friends. It's the kind of coincidence that happens all the time. Coincidence is just coincidence. There's nothing to be made of it. And it's only a mild one at that, but it makes a connection between two strangers. I tell him how Steve gave me water and wrote a story about my experience.

"Yeah, Steve is a writer," he says.

"I still have the card he gave me." This comment prompts the man to dig out one of his own cards. He only has one left and part of it has been torn off. But his name is still on it. I look like a bedraggled homeless man standing beside the professionally dressed man, reading his card. It says Mac Bumpus is Vice President of First Jackson Bank. He's also friendly. So, I'll remember Jasper for Mac and Steve. And, of course I don't forget the Seventh-Day Adventist Church at the base of the mountain, the place where I had the best sleep I've had in a while.

I leave out of the Jasper Quick Stop with some sweet stuff to eat and aim toward Kimball, five miles away. The shredded soles on my feet still ache. I didn't pull my shoes off last night. They've been on a long time. My walk is still a plod. I drift along munching on a granola bar. Last time I passed along here, two years ago, I was enough ahead of today's pace to be still in nighttime. I was munching on a polish sausage pickled in vinegar. I walked pass road-kill I couldn't even see. It was stinking enough it nearly made me puke the sausage. I haven't eaten a pickled polish sausage since. Come to think of it, I don't know why I was eating it that night, maybe to satisfy a need for protein. Carbohydrates would have been a better choice than a stick of grease.

Kimball clutter begins to pick up. I'm maybe a mile from the Super-8, the race hotel where most of us stayed the night before we took the chartered bus trip to Union City on the far end of the course.

"Hello, Dallas." I turn to look. John Price has come up behind me. John is the sage of this race, the one who posted maps of the course on the Internet, free for everyone. He's run this race six times. I believe he told me two years ago. That now comes to eight, not counting this time. Twice, after finishing he turned back and went over the course again, in the opposite direction. A tornado in West Tennessee interrupted his return trip once. He's crossed North America on foot twice, ocean to ocean. This is routine stuff for him.

"I wasn't expecting you, John, I thought you'd gone on."

He could have if he'd wanted to. He's not sweating it, just taking it easy. Like Johnny, he's walking, but he's walking well. So, I let him go on. In fact, I couldn't not let him go on if I wanted to.

"You look strong. Keep it up," wishing him the usual running stuff. So, we go through Kimball in tandem, his lead on me stretching. By the time I reach Super-8, he's well ahead and will soon be passing under I-24.

Kimball is a nowhere place, little more than a spot on the map between Jasper and South Pittsburg. Then I-24 came through that spot and made an interchange. Now Kimball is a big parking lot surrounded by hotels and restaurants. It looks like a place without a history. There is, though, I should note, a cemetery here, across the road from Super-8. Our finish line ledge we call The Rock, is just fourteen miles from this Super-8. I'm hoping to return soon. Save a bed for me, Super-8.

I follow U.S. 72, passing under I-24. Soon the road becomes a pedestrian's nightmare: howling traffic, the roar of big trucks and small cars alike, curving on-ramps and off-ramps, dividing medians and concrete shoulders abutting tall concrete retaining walls. The hard artificial topography amplifies the noise to a cacophony that makes the world seem alien, hostile and scary, a world gone mad, inimical to soul and body—at least if you are afoot and not in a vehicle. And you think, *My God, what have we done?* I trundle along with an aching back, trying to stretch out the pain and trying hard not to become trapped in the maze and myself turned into road kill.

A Chevy pickup sets on the concrete shoulder ahead, the man in it waiting, watching in his side rear view. I walk up to his open window, and he looks at me, a ruddy round-faced man.

"Are you okay?" The question is becoming popular.

"Uh, yeah, I'm fine, just tired."

"Well, you had your arms over your head and you were wobbling."

"My back was hurting. I was trying to stretch it while I walked."

Then I tell him about the race, where we started and when, how much sleep I've lost, and that I'm the oldest to attempt it unsupported. He fairly sputters in awe and amazed wonderment. I don't get the idea he doubts my tale at all. It's just that it's an activity he's never encountered, and it jars him. Then he drives on. I'm on the concrete alone again beside the howling traffic.

Half a mile later, an SUV pulls over ahead, same deal. It's the same man again. He has changed vehicles and brought his wife back so she can see me, as if she would never have believed him otherwise. He steps out of the car and begins making my picture, circling for angles, and peppering me with questions—my name, age, where I live and so on. He wants me to talk to his wife. I lean through the door he left open, greet her, gently shake her hand and we have a little chat.

These are not runners. The gentleman is a heavyset man, round body, round head, red face, short legs and decked out in a Hawaiian shirt. But he's jovial, laughs a lot, and I like both him and his demure wife. He's just glimpsed a world he didn't know existed on this earth and found that people do things he'd never dreamed. And to share it, he brought his wife to see me. I'll take it as a compliment. They drive away, having no idea how my raw feet are burning.

The road to New Hope crosses the Tennessee River on what's called the Blue Bridge, called that because it is indeed blue. I approach it with a reverent sense of respect. I used to make my living designing bridges. My bridges are all penny-ante compared to this one—a single span, trussed overhead arch, the roadway slung on cables below it. I have to stop long enough to make a picture. I drift lightly across it, looking up at the blue steel lattice, inspecting the cable connections up close, a chance you'd not realize or think of in driving across.

This is the second time I've crossed the Tennessee on this run, once in West Tennessee, where it flows north toward Kentucky, and now here, where it angles southwest toward Alabama. But I can't linger. I have to finish this business.

New Hope is just a strung out country community. You aren't quite sure when it starts or when it ends. What can you see or care about, if you are so sleepy? There are modest houses, a church, what looks to be a community center that might've once been a school—back a long time ago when there were small community schools, before they were consolidated in the towns. It sets back to the left and there are shade trees and I think: *I could find a place to sleep there.* I dismiss that thought. Got to keep going. What else do we have? A market, where I buy two bottles of water from a slender, taciturn man.

A charming thing happened here, when I passed through two years ago. I saw a family on the front porch of a shaded frame house. I wasn't so sleepy or aching that day. I walked up to the porch to see if I could refill my water bottles.

"Oh, no! We've got cold water in the refrigerator." He disappeared into the house yelling for his wife. Soon they both came to the door carrying three bottles of water. The two kids stood looking on. They'd seen some other runners pass, but they didn't know what was happening, had no idea they'd come from Missouri until I told them. They listened to my story in hushed awe. They were astonished, maybe more so because of my advanced age. Even grandma stood listening behind the screen door, demurely holding it open a few inches to get a better look.

"Amazing. God bless," the gentlemen said.

I couldn't easily carry three bottles.

"I think I'll drink this one here and carry the other two with me."

They all watched in silent and reverent amazement as I turned the bottle up and drank it in a single gurgling pull, slung the droplets out, screwed the lid back on and handed the empty back to him in one flourish.

"I'll leave the empty with you." The man reached out to take it.

"Amazing. God bless," he said a second time, his face blanched in sincerity.

Drinking it like that sounds like a grand theatric gesture, but in fact I was thirsty, I couldn't carry three bottles and I wanted them to know I appreciated their generosity. That was two years ago.

I trudge through this place differently this time. A

city park is not what you'd expect in New Hope. But here it is more an open field than anything else, but the sign says it's the New Hope City Park. It lies sweltering in July's heat. No one is here, nor is it easy to see why anyone would want to be here—except me. Maybe I could sleep there if it were the dark of night and the sun wasn't pressing down. But the timing is wrong.

The insistent need for sleep never lets up. Soon the road climbs and disappears over a sharp crest and just before that crest a paved driveway goes left. It immediately turns to gravel, but before it does, there's a spot of shade. I glance down the driveway. No house is in sight and a wire is stretched across it where it goes into the woods. That tells me it's a mere farm access road, seldom used. I won't be run over here by a motorist rushing to work. I throw down my pack, my pillow, and stretch out, feet toward the road, like up on the plateau.

But it's no good. I'm in plain sight and too close to the road. Soon a car stops with the old question I hear so much: "Are you okay?" and I lie again saying yes, having time for a short lie but not for a longer truth—the truth is too complicated and serves no useful purpose for either of us. After my brief lie the car goes on. Soon, I realize I must also.

Now Don Winkley passes me, walking strongly, alternating the walk with a gentle shuffle-like run that ultramarathoners use. His passing doesn't change my position since he's a supported runner. His is a story to admire, once finishing first in the unsupported category. He's seventy-seven years old now and the only runner keeping me from being the oldest in this race—although that still leaves me as the oldest unsupported runner. So, yeah, that's good. Or it's terrible, depending on your view. I don't have much opinion on the matter just now. It just is.

Don's wearing a white shirt and white beard, as I am. And he's my height, so we must look like twins. We move along together chatting, the usual runner stuff. I know I have to let him go, so I tell him good luck and that he looks strong. And by God he does. At seventy-seven he yet evinces strength. I watch the smoothness, the fluidity, of his motion as he pulls on ahead, his broad back, arm swing and stride. He is yet a man of vitality and strength. You can take encouragement from that. On this rolling curvy road, he soon disappears from view.

You could get killed out here. This is a narrow road. It undulates and curves creating blind spots. Up ahead is such a place. The road disappears over a crest at the same time it curves left, putting me on the inside once I get there. Don Winkley's crew member has parked his car in the grass on the right.

I'm on the left side of the road, as a pedestrian should be. Sometimes that's a bad idea. Like now. The pavement crowds hard against a bank with no benefit of even ditch or shoulder. A pickup pulling a trailer is going to track hard inside and there will be no place for the hapless runner to go—except scramble quickly up the bank if he can. Don's man is up there and he knows this. He is yelling at me and making sweeping arm waves telling me to get on the other side. Finally, I get the idea and change to the right edge. When I reach the safety of his parking place on the outside of the curve, I stop to chat. He can't offer me drink or food. I'd lose my standing as an unsupported runner. Safety advice is another matter.

"It's too dangerous being on the inside in that blind place."

Standing across the road from there, I can see how right he is. It's worse than I could have known. I thank him, and we stand chatting. Suddenly he starts. A pickup and trailer rig sweep through the curve, its wind whipping the grass where I would have been.

"See, that's what I was talking about," he says. Demonstration made, lesson learned.

The waters of Nickajack Lake are on my left, mostly out of sight. Up ahead the waters cross under the road and form a cove on my right. That's a good landmark. Just past it is where I take another two-lane to the right and start my climb up Sand Mountain. It's a hill with steep sides and ledges you can fall off of, including the one where this race officially ends. With six or eight more miles to go, I don't know, I start my trudge upward. Going slow but still going, painful and slow, but I think I'll get there.

I leave Tennessee as I climb this hill, and start traveling in Alabama. Half way up, a young man in a white Ranger stops. "You need a ride?"

"Yeah, I do..." I say, thinking he's kidding, then suddenly realizing he's serious, "but I can't take it. I'm in a race. It started in Kentucky and it ends at Castle Rock. I'm nearly there. Thanks though."

This unexpected statement comes from an old man with a white beard. The generous young man looks stunned. He searches for the right response and finally says simply, "Well, okay." Road Angel thwarted. He drives on up the hill.

Going up this hill you are embedded in the wooded scenery. Trees hang over. It's like a trail except for the asphalt ribbon you run on. My head becomes a busy place, full of memories. That helps push out the pain. At a pull-out two years ago there was an old man with his tractor and bush hog. I stopped to talk a minute. I felt good that day. His bush hog was broken, he grumbled. That's the trouble with bush hogs. They stay broke a lot. The old gentleman probably had no idea why I was there, how I'd materialized, as it were, out of nowhere.

Joshua Holmes came down the hill in his white Chevy truck. Diane Bolton was with him. They came just to check on me and make some pictures. He'd finished a couple days earlier. Diane had finished during the night. A handsome lady in any case, she'd had time to clean up and put on a perky dress. Iconic image: She stood at an overlook, Nickajack surrounded by green mountains in the background reaching her arms spread wide to the sky and smiling big. "Mine! All mine!" her gesture said. And her gesture was right. She'd earned it.

The thick edge of the pavement disappears in the uncut grass. I should be watching rather than remembering. I step on the edge. Which so stabs my foot with added pain that I jerk the weight off of it. That throws me toward the shoulder and I go over the side, sliding down the mountain in loose dirt, gravel and scree, rushing like an avalanche, snatching out vines and weeds, anything for braking, trying to stop, trying to stay upright and wondering if I am going to arrest the slide.

Then, amazingly, I do stop, still upright, both aching feet in notches they've dug in the hillside. I stand resting a few seconds hanging onto vines, glad I didn't slide further. I could've gone way down. It could've been tragic.

I have to climb back up. That means pressing extra hard on my raw feet, and I pull on the vines to help. I now check those vines I'm pulling, figuring to see they'll be poison ivy. But I'm lucky. In a place where you'd expect the stuff everywhere, there's none here. Twice lucky. I get back to the road and brush off the dirt, glad I don't have poison ivy juice all over my hands.

Sonofabitch! I nearly fell off this goddamned mountain!

I'm not sleepy anymore.

Upon inspection the pavement edge reveals a contributing factor: it has *two* edges. There's the edge of the original pavement and a second edge of re-pavement. The re-pavement edge stops six inches short of the original pavement. It's likely the top edge that threw me off balance. I need to pay attention. I continue on, wary now.

It takes over and hour to top out. Then I keep going and I keep going. Now there are pastures and scattered houses. There's a name or number or something for the road I need to turn left on. I wonder if I've missed it. Seems I should have come to it by now. But there's a definite landmark, a very unlikely one. I made a note of it on my map two years ago, and I still remember. A white sign, maybe four by six, that says:

BENCH OF DESPAIR

PARTY HARDY

The sign advertises party merchandise and services, not something you'd think anyone in this rural community would be looking to buy. Anyway, merchandising aside, I'm looking for the party hardy sign. When I find it, the road will be there. Somewhere after this junction I'll leave Alabama and enter Georgia.

It's a welcome sight when I find it, the party hardy sign. I turn left. I am near finishing 314 miles—or one hundred π, as we joke. This little rolling road shoots like a bee-line right into Castle Rock. I remember this road fondly for how strong I was the last time I ran the race. I was *running*, feeling good, not trudging on raw feet like now. This is how I blithely described that experience in a Facebook post:

Finally, on top of Sand Mountain, I ran like a sprite, turned left at the Party Hardy sign I'd marked on my map to help me spot the turn, kept on running over the two lane rollers into Georgia and Castle Rock and still running onto the dirt farm road and thru the soy bean fields finally into the woods and still running as I approached the rock ledge when they started yelling for me to slow down and Carl Laniak got his hands on me, afraid I was going to sail right on over the edge into oblivion and walked me up to a bump on the rock ledge a foot from the sheer hundred-foot drop and said, "That bump is the finish," and when I put my foot on it he yelled to Laz up under the tent roof, "That's it!" And Laz answered back "That's 8 days 5 hours, 34 minutes and 11 seconds," and I hunkered down to make a picture of the bump looking for the precise place where 314 miles or 100π ended so I could mark it with my knife and Carl said, "I can't tell you exactly since π is an irrational number."

This time I'll not go so swiftly to Castle Rock and through the ranch and through the woods and out to the ledge. But I do remember how that was. I walk along today on burning feet and gaze at the houses I pass.

At an older frame house an emaciated old lady is out with a hoe working in the July heat, digging up the grass that laps over the edge of her concrete walk. Long-suffering pioneer stock, the woman likely lives alone, and work is what she knows. She reminds me of my mom. Momma had a stroke at age seventy-nine on a hot June day while working outside with a swing blade. She could have left those weeds, like this lady could leave the grass.

The old lady looks up as I pass. I wave and say, "It's hot out here today. Be careful." In reply, she makes a tiny wave but doesn't speak. I wouldn't expect her to.

A car comes from behind. I turn to look. It's a runner, one that's already finished. He's just hanging out up here. He slows to a stop, and grins, a big kidder.

"Want a ride?"

"You'd fix me up, wouldn't you?"

He knows I know I'm nearly finished and that I'm not likely to be in anything but a good mood, all the pains and hurt notwithstanding. He rides on toward the ledge where I'll see him again soon.

The curved stone parapets on each side of the road announce Castle Rock, like a gateway. Gateway to what, I wonder? So far as I can see nothing but a big farm. A one-lane, paved drive lined with shade trees continues on. Welcome me, Castle Rock. I've been traveling a long way to get to you. But I don't enter the rustic kingdom just yet because Don Winkley and his crewman are standing here in front of their white van. Don's finished. They're headed out, but stopped here for the memories, I suppose. I stop too. We've played footsie for four days, for 150 miles. We need a ceremonial goodbye before they drive off this mountain. We laugh and talk. It's been a vivid experience. I turn to go, and then Don says something strange.

"I admire you...but I don't want to duplicate you."

I don't understand his meaning. It's an enigma. He can't admire me for doing this despite my age. He's older. Nor for my speed. He beat me. Nor for going unaided. He did once and beat everyone. It's an enigma I carry into Castle Rock.

I pass my car setting in the field to the right under the power lines, parked there nine days ago. Then I turn left and follow the tractor road. Joshua Holmes made an iconic photo of me entering here two years ago. It looked like big country, a lonely runner on a long road.

The soybean field of two years ago has turned into a cornfield. A wall of dense stalks high as a house on either side of the tractor road. It's like going through a roofless tunnel. My aching feet pad the powdery dirt, stirring little clouds of dust. Soon now…

The dusty tractor road stretches on through the corn. Soon it enters the woods. It's rather curvy through the trees. I keep looking, expecting to see the shade thin out, to see a few cars parked there where Laz, Carl, John and others wait. The wooded road is longer than I remember from two years ago, maybe, as John will later note, because I was running then instead of trudging.

Eventually, the trees open a bit. Now the cars are setting there. The rocks hurt my feet. The men under the canopy tent watch me trudge toward the rock ledge. Carl comes up to escort me, moving between me and the edge. They can see how shaky I am, how weak. I can make no pretense of strength. It took all I had to get to here. Carl has to brace me a few times as I stumble on the pain-causing rocks.

Now we stand on the ledge, Carl watching me like a nervous father. I'm glad he is. I reach out my foot and touch the bump on the rock that marks the finish line, just a foot from the precipice. A hundred-foot free-fall waits there. Carl yells up to Laz, that I've finished. And I don't even care about the finish time. Instead, I stand looking out, north into the mouth of the Sequatchie Valley, at the waters of Nickajack, looking into Tennessee, at Tennessee scenery. Before leaving the ledge—which everyone calls The Rock—I find the energy to make a photo of my index finger pressing down on the rock's bump, the finish, the ultimate finish. Carl hovers, flanking me and the edge. He's a tall strong guy. I turn and look at the decrepit bench setting behind us, faded from long weather exposure.

"It looks pretty rickety," I offer. I'm thinking about sitting on it.

"Yeah, it's not safe," Carl agrees. "Well, you might could sit on it if you sit easy on this end."

The bench sets looking toward Tennessee, overlooking the far distance from the ledge. But I decide against sitting, which is likely a relief to Carl. He'll like it better once I get away from this ledge. Carl braces me as I stumble up the short slope and to the tent, where Laz, the man who offered me the joke ride, and a couple others I don't know sit in the shade under the awning. They offer me the yellow bag chair. They like to call the color "gold," and refer to the chair as the throne. It's where a recent finisher gets to sit for a while, King for a while.

"We got water, Coke or beer," one says. That's no choice, and I ask for the beer. He pops the lid off and hands me a bottle of Samuel Adams.

My official time recorded to exacting precision by Laz is 8 days, 10 hours, 9 minutes, 10 seconds. Which is five hours slower than I was last time. You get older, you get slower, but I'd thought I could beat my last time.

I sit drinking, resting, and we chat a bit. It feels good to sit at rest, to not move, not need to move. Laz sits easy quartering on my right. A fritz beard spreads over his collar. There's a piece of history I remember, and I'm the only one here who could know it. Laz should be interested.

In addition to this one, Laz has created other iconic races. The Barkley Marathons is so hard it's been written about at the *New York Times*. Only a handful of runners have ever managed to finish it. The Strolling Jim forty-mile ultramarathon, which I've run twice, at Wartrace, Tennessee is decades old. When I first heard about it, I thought the race was likely named for a local eccentric—Laz would qualify—who spent a lot of time hoofing it along the road.

I was wrong. I didn't know anything about walking horse history. Strolling Jim, in fact, was the first World Champion Walking Horse. His grave is behind the Walking Horse Hotel in Wartrace where the ultramarathon named for him starts and ends. So, the Strolling Jim race is named for a dead horse, one deceased since 1939.

So, I tell Laz the story: There is in my little town of Cookeville a man named Wade Odom. He is a few years older than even I am. I see him frequently, and I first met him at a football game when I was wearing a Boston Marathon jacket. He came up to me and asked if I'd run Boston. Of course I had. Then he asked me if I'd run the Strolling Jim race. Yes, I'd done that, too. He was interested because he'd grown up in Wartrace. Then Wade said something breathtaking.

"I used to ride Strolling Jim for his cool-down after Mr. Carothers gave him his workout."

Wade was a little boy then, but Mr. Carothers would let him ride the horse.

So, here is Wade Odom, a live man walking around in my town that I know, a man who is a living link to history, a live connection to the famous horse that died seventy-six years ago.

History comes alive. The story fascinates me. Sitting there on the Golden Throne, I conclude my story to Laz.

"Since you created a race named after Strolling Jim, I

figured you'd be interested in that story."

But I am wrong. Laz shows only mild interest. He makes a cursory remark, more a gesture than speech, and then the conversation drifts on to other topics. Living near Wartrace, maybe Laz has heard enough Strolling Jim lore to make mine trite. I'm not offended, of course, just surprised. It seems out of character for a man who is, himself, a vessel of so many stories. Laz is tired, too, from hanging out up here.

Still, it's pleasant to sit sunken into the bag chair, sipping on the beer. Soon, though, John Price decides to go. He looks at me.

"You need a ride?"

Actually, that would be nice. My car has waited for me over nine days now. It sets about a half mile back. It seems more like a mile in my present condition.

I follow John wearily to his car, stumbling on the rocks. They hurt my feet, cruelly. John sits down behind the wheel. From outside, I throw my pack down in the back seat and start to get in the shotgun seat. Laz has followed to see us off. He stands in my way, holding the door open. He looks at me.

"Why don't you let John take you on to the hotel? He could bring you back to your car in the morning."

"What!? Over one beer?"

"It's not the beer. You're having a hard time. He could bring you back in the morning."

"I'm stumbling around because my feet hurt. There's nothing wrong with my mind."

"I know, but that'll make it hard to drive your car

down the mountain."

I start to say that I drive a Prius. It takes very little pressure on the pedals. Besides driving down the mountain isn't half as dangerous as trudging up it on foot, as I have just done. I have food and clean clothes in my car. For days I've been looking forward to a shower and clean clothes, driving to Cracker Barrel and having a big supper. But Laz is worried about me and he's made up his mind. Still holding the door open, he leans in and tells John,

"Take him on to the hotel, John."

"To the hotel?"

"Yeah, to the hotel."

I hesitate. I stand here in the first person. They're talking about me in the third person. I'm cut out of the decision-making. Laz is not wrong. But I'm determined and stubborn. I want my car tonight, the Cracker Barrel tonight. So, when Laz says, "Yeah, to the hotel," I make a first-person decision.

"I guess I'll walk then."

I reach in to retrieve my pack. It's not a bluff. It's just what I'm going to do, one more trudge to make before I can finish this adventure, back through the woods, through the corn. It's hard to walk, but I can do it. It won't take long. Laz still stands holding the door. He changes his mind.

"Take him to his car, John."

"To the car?"

"Yeah, to the car."

With that reversal, I hesitate again, another decision to make. I agree, I decide. I ease my pack back into the seat and take the shotgun seat. John and I head out. My car sets directly underneath the high-tension power lines, patiently waiting where I left it nine days ago.

A poignant meeting: As I'm heading down the road, leaving The Rock, suddenly here comes a runner. I drive slightly past before I realize: It's Jameelah! I'd last seen her in Linden days ago, when she was struggling with foot blisters. I stop my car and jump out to yell for her. There she is running brave and hard down County Highway 132, just two miles from the finish, and I know nothing on this earth can stop her now. She looks back and waves. It's an enduring image I take away, likely the last glimpse I'll ever have of the brave woman, I figure.

I drive on toward the Party Hardy sign. Then, there's Fred, my buddy on the long trudge across the plateau in the middle of last night. He's just made the Party Hardy turn and he has a friend who turns out to be Gilbert Gray, a man I've not talked to before. I stop to chat.

"You look a lot better than you did last night," I tell Fred.

"Ahh, you were complaining more than me," he says. And he's probably right about that. It took falling asleep in the Driveway to Nowhere to stop my whining.

Chapter Eleven

Lord of the Flies

At the Kimball Super-8, I check into a room. The four-teen-mile drive down the mountain and through Good Hope was uneventful, as I'd expected. Oddly, I seem to have transcended sleepiness, to have forgotten about it. It's no longer a part of my being, as if I've been cured of it. I haven't been drowsy since I fell off the road going up Sand Mountain.

My room is full of flies. Not one or two, a room full buzzing like bees. Apparently, the housekeeping staff left the door open while they cleaned and the flies sought out the cool space. I don't have a fly swatter. The best I can do is to grab a hotel towel and swat them with it. Generally, I wait until one alights on the big mirror over the sink. There's always something. It takes time and being on my feet, while I desperately want to shower and go eat. The towel is not as controllable as a swatter, so sometimes it takes several tries to kill a single fly. I make progress with the project, but each time I think I've killed the last one, another one shows up. Finally I quit, hoping I've killed them all.

My luck only gets worse. As I step out of the shower, the raw bottom of my foot slips. I come crashing down, banging the side of the tub and the shower doors. I'm not sure there's anything in the room I don't hit. It's chaos. When I finally quit falling I end up sitting in the floor hugging the toilet. I sit dazed, afraid to move, wondering what damage I've done. I finished Vol State but I'm still in trouble.

I have to move. Nobody's going to come in here and pick me up. So, I begin to rise up, bracing first on the toilet. My raw feet against the hard tile floor hurt. I slip again. This time my bottom crashes down hard on the edge of the toilet seat and the pain shoots upward. The bruise it makes goes deep. It will finally erupt into an oozing sore that takes a doctor and four weeks to heal. I sit there in pain, like somebody drove a bridge nail into my right hip. At least I'm in a sitting position and a little higher than I was the last time I tried to get up. I'm getting up in stages, it seems. I make it to a standing position on the next attempt.

Once I get dressed, it's too late and too far to walk to the Cracker Barrel, and I don't want to give up my parking place in front of the room. Instead, I opt for the Waffle House, just half a block down the walk. I begin the same painful trudge I used to finish the race, gingerly hobbling along. Suddenly, Laz appears in the parking lot. He's come off the mountain too. He sees me and walks over to the sidewalk. I expect he's being friendly, concerned that

I might have hard feelings about the disagreement on the mountain. If so, he need not be. Mentally and spiritually, I'm at ease. It's my body that's broken. I tell him about falling in the bathroom. That is an opening.

"Well, see, something like that was what I was worried about up on the mountain."

"I know."

Confessing the fall is the right thing to do. It validates his concern and vindicates his position on the mountain. It's charitable. It's what a diplomat would do. We part. I'm glad we met. I hope we both are.

There is a market between the Waffle House and Super-8. On the way back to my room after supper, I stop in for a pack of Miller Lite. Back in the room, I discover, there's still a fly buzzing around. I ignore it. I sit on the bed and pour a Miller into a hotel glass, take a sip and set the glass on the night stand.

Twelve hours later, I wake up, warm beer setting there, room lights full on, hotel fly still buzzing around. Its hairy feet had probably walked on my lips. I remember nothing. That's twelve hours for which I can offer no account, no dreams, no trips to the bathroom, nothing at all. Total nothingness, a blank space void of memories or tales. It'd been a total blackout, like at the Jasper church—except three times longer.

It's too late for breakfast. The hotel buffet is closed. I check out, grab a cup of hotel coffee for the console. As I'm walking back to the room, an SUV rolls across the parking lot. Give or take ten seconds and we never meet. But there we are in the narrow window of a few seconds. We do meet. The driver's window goes down. I look in. It's Fred and Gilbert and someone else in the back. I look closer and she speaks. It's Jameelah.

I grab at the door handle. "Let me in there!"

She jerks the door open and jumps out. We hug. Emotion pours out. We relive the run. She and I shared some taunt moments early on. Our runs had been in jeopardy on the very first day—our health, too. Now, here, nine days later, we meet again. It seems like providence. We've made it. We've *all* made it. Meeting again is lucky. Parting is sad but hopeful. Maybe we'll meet again, maybe here, maybe somewhere, maybe...

It's now so late for breakfast, I decide to skip it. I drive up the Sequatchie Valley and stop at the Dunlap Restaurant, a home-cooking joint I visit when I'm passing through Dunlap at meal time. They cook their own turnip greens. I saw crates of the raw leaves stacked at the back door once. And, they peel their own potatoes. Here I shall eat. I had apricot cobbler here once, a dish so rare I've never seen it even listed on the menu at any other restaurant. Apricots are expensive. If this sounds like an ad for the restaurant, it shows why, even though hungry, I was willing to wait until I got here.

The restaurant is crowded this Saturday. I take a bar stool and I know what to order: water, coffee and milk with a veggie plate of pinto beans, turnip greens, potato salad, fried okra, corn bread and a garden salad with blue cheese. It sounds like a lot to the waitress, a savvy dark-headed woman used to slinging plate lunches.

"You want a to-go box with that?"

"No."

"I bet you will."

It was a bet she would've lost. But how could she have known?